THE CRYSTAL SOUL PRIESTESS

A Crystalline Journey of Ascension

Rhosalaria Gwyneth Robbins-Cox

Copyright © 2021 Gwyneth Cox

All rights reserved

No part of this book may be reproduced, or stored in a retrieval system, or transmitted in any form or by any means, electronic, mechanical, photocopying, recording, or otherwise, without express written permission of the publisher.

ISBN 979-8476343127

Cover design by: Pia Tohveri PhD
Piatohveri.com
Additional illustrations by Kara McGlinn

To all those with open hearts and eyes to see beyond the illusory world.

To the love of the Lemurian Elders and the Starbeings who guide us

To all my family, friends and teachers

The Crystal Soul Priestess

The collective of hue-manity, and our Divine Mother Earth are at a pivotal point in our evolution.

At this time now we feel the call of our Soul's presence, a time for which we have long awaited and that which we incarnated to be a part of. To become the Crystalline Light Beings that we innately always were and to be part of the great unfolding of the Cosmic alignment and return to Love.

These pages are free from being the 'usual' kind of crystal information appendix. Within these pages lies an energetic narrative of the nature of our Soul story here as hue-man beings and the connection to the crystal energies of Lemuria and their wisdom.

Much of the information here was channelled beginning in June 2017 onwards. As you read the channels written here in italics, please take time to absorb their feeling for the words have been brought through from the beings at the Heart of Andromeda and the Lemurian Elders with Love for Hue-manity on Earth/Heart for the purpose of assisting the divine integration of Love and Light that is our destined journey of consciousness.

INTRODUCTION

This book is a culmination of my work as a Crystal Healer and my experience in this lifetime and others as a Priestess and a Soul Medium. The writings for this book are given in co-creation and channel from Divine Mother Source, Lemurian Elders, the Universal Heart of the Akasha and the consciousness at the Heart of Andromeda.

In political correctness, the word Priestess contains within it the word Priest. The word Priestess means someone who serves the Divine Light and Source, acting as a conduit for Love, healing and Light in Service to Hue-manity.

The gathering of channel and writing began for this book almost four years ago. During this extended time of transformation and change the original blueprint for this book has moved through the words originally given in channel to be pieced together into something that is hopefully of inspiration to others in the changing times we are now experiencing.

The process for writing this has been a reflection in part of my own transformation through the ongoing ascension process. It is my personal experience that anything that is co-created happens through a need to complete a process that is happening both on a personal level and within the Collective of hue-manity.

With that in mind I would like to say that this book is for everyone who recognises that being upon planet Earth is a spiritual journey of ascension and integration with Divine Love. It is a journey of individuation for the Soul. We are each of us greater beings of Soul Consciousness experiencing a life on Earth now and we all have a mission to fulfil and a part to play in the great unfolding of what is often called the coming of the new Golden Age of New Earth. Thank you for reading that which I am sharing here with you - it is given with the highest divine love and in honour and appreciation of all hue-man Souls. I hope also that it will resonate deeply with your own inner knowledge and wisdom offering inspiration to you along the divine pathway of your Soul's journey and remembering.

The crystal reflections contained within this book are my own reflections to help inspire you to connect to crystalline energies. Crystals are a manifestation of Light upon the Earth, record keepers of our Journey as hue-man beings and the journey of the planet itself. Within each crystal being lie the keys to ascension freedom and your journey home. Free from being a crystal healing book per se, I hope that the combination of Soul connection and crystal connection will help you to remember who you truly are and to recognise more of your soul's true blueprint manifesting upon Earth now.

So what first inspired the writing of this book? Here I shall share with you briefly the process that awakened the inspiration within.

In August 2016, staying at my mother's house, I woke up and experienced a spontaneous download of information. It was an immense and intense feeling. A rush of power and connectedness which felt a little scary. The energy continued to flow and I asked where it was coming from. The answer came that the energy was coming from Andromeda and as an Andromedan Starseed I was receiving healing and channel from the higher Beings at the Heart of Andromeda to help me feel 'at ease and reconnected to my home.' A steady and clear channel persisted for two whole days and I sensed that this connection to the Light and to another dimension was proof to me in Soul that there is so much more to us as hue-man beings. I wondered at times if the information was real and was plunged deeply into the process of trusting - but when opening to channel the feeling I sensed was one of the purest heartfelt Love. A feeling that is not so often and readily perceived upon the heaviness of this Earth Dimension. For two whole days I downloaded information constantly, I felt the presence of the Andromedan consciousness answering many questions and it became a game almost - my husband would ask me a question and

I would receive the answer instantly from channel. After two days, the strength of the channel receded a little as the Andromedans became a little distant once more - but I understood that they had come to open a doorway, to help me sense that my Soul was seeded from the heart of Andromeda and also to bring comfort, a greater sense of my purpose, a Soul healing and to ultimately help open more doorways. I understood and took comfort from the fact that so many times on Earth I had felt 'out of place', mis-aligned from an emotional perspective of being in the human body with all its 'conditioning.'

The freedom of love and to experience love in its purest form is the essence of Andromeda - innocence, en-joyment and fulfilment through co-creation which is at the heart of Andromedan way of life.

Shortly after this experience my husband's son fell ill with a brain tumour and we were plunged into a difficult time of experiencing many feelings of hope, devastation and finally grief. After nine months my step son sadly passed away. Throughout this time, our lives went on hold. Things began to fall apart and afterwards we began a process of letting go deeply, shedding layers upon layers of emotional attachments.

When we witness the passing of a Soul, it is a beautiful experience as well as being immensely sad . It feels as though a part of you goes with them and we may feel fully the absolute Love of Source. We became, I became changed irrevocably.

Before the funeral, I was scheduled to attend a Festival as a workshop leader rather reluctantly as I felt sad at leaving my husband alone at such a difficult time. However, on going to the festival and to fulfil my role as a workshop leader, I met a beautiful Soul with whom I knew instantly I had a connection to. We spent time talking and remembering our connection. A few weeks later I heard her sing a Soul song which immediately opened another doorway for me which enabled me to access the Universal Heart of the Akasha. Through Source and Soul connection I saw through the multidimensions of my own Soul and felt a deep, deep knowing and connection to the wisdoms of Lemuria. I held my Lemurian Seed Crystal of which I have had in my possession for so many years I can't even remember where it came from, but I understood that I had found it years ago in readiness for this time and In holding the crystal I began channelling information which forms at least part of this book.

I had been given the name 'The Crystal Soul Priestess' a few months before but at that time, had no idea what that meant or what it was supposed to be. It took a year for life to unravel, to trust and allow things to fully fall into place as well as deep Soul searching, processing, moving home, letting go, and huge transformation before this book and its meaning became any way near complete.

Why Lemuria? It is in our understanding of the nature of our multidimensional Soul that the first life upon Earth was in what was known as Lemuria or Mu. We were at that time ethereal beings with a strong active connection to the Earth as well as the stars from whence we came. Many souls are now re-membering the energies and dreaming of Lemuria which echoes back through the timelines and dimensions of the soul and the collective, remembering the Love and reverence for Mother Earth. What a sense of privilege it is to be upon the Earth and to work with Her energies at this time!

This book is a co-creation of the purest Love in gratitude and appreciation for Earth and Divine Mother Source through the divine manifestation of Love in Crystalline form within the Earth and the Crystalline Light within each of us here.

As you read, allow your heart to open to receive the words perhaps as some ancient fictitious story which shall unfold to reveal the sovereignty and truth lying deep within your soul's remembering.

With blessings of Light and Love

Rhosalaria

THE REMEMBERING

Lemuria. A place that exists within the essence, the blueprint of our Soul as hue-man beings.

In some senses, a place that is in our extra sensory memory, a garden of Eden - a place of bliss held within the dreaming of our consciousness. We can best remember the energies of Lemuria by connecting into the energies of our higher heart. Therein lies the True Heart, the Celestial tree as it is known to some, a centre for bliss. The Higher Heart, Ananda Khanda, Dolphin Chakra is located where the physical Thymus gland is. Often used in EFT and tapping, when we engage with this centre we are awakening the deepest memories of Bliss. This is the Bliss Chakra that is also the portal into the Heart Chakra itself.

Prior to the genetic alteration of DNA that took place in Atlantean times orchestrated and overseen by other races including the Pleiadians, we may remember the legacy of the original hue-man races upon Earth who came from the Stars.

These celestial races or the first hue-man originators wanted to place the memory of the true nature and the sovereignty of the hue-man being within the geometric codes held within the crystalline forms inside the Earth.

Thousands of our linear years ago, the Lemurian people knew that a time would come on Earth for the ascension of hue-manity. Many years would pass in darkness and in diminishment of the true rainbow Light that Hue-manity innately carried. Many years of slavery and admonishment of the Truth have passed. The information that had been lost and hidden away could be accessed through the Light codes of consciousness embedded in crystalline form both within the crystal beings of the Earth and within the crystalline patterning of our very own hue-man structure. Here is the beginning of the remembering of lemuria in channel:

'I am Rhosalaria - Lady of the rose pink Light - Crystal Priestess of Love. I am in this remembering who I am within the beautiful energies of Lemuria.

There once existed upon this Earth, great Temples of Light - created of Crystal. Their purpose was to house the great crystals which received information and sacred protection in connection with the Galactic Beings in the Cosmos.

Divine Source is held sacred as is Divine Feminine and Divine Masculine, in being an indivisible partnership of such. She, Divine Source, as Creatress from the Highest Source of Light. She is vibration, She is Love, She is Purest Form. Divine Masculine as Her partner, Her consort and together they seek to manifest Love on Earth. They are One with each other and within each of us, all life, in Divine Unity as holographic expressions of Love and Light.

There is no need for struggle in creation, for thought is everything. We have only but to think or imagine and it shall form into Being. We are in divine alignment. This has been corrupted and abused through the times of slavery. But this is how the Crystal Priestesses would work. For all vibration and thought is stored within the crystals upon the Earth. As timeline dimensions have shifted and corruption of thought manifests into darkness in this dimension, destruction came. Love has been stored within the Light contained in the crystals of the Earth. In this way, every divine expression of Love and Manifestation could be stored. Crystals could then be used to heal and to help us re-member who we are in the days of returning to the Golden Age.

And that as the dawning of that age comes upon us - many of these crystallisations of Love will disappear in their physical form and we shall become crystalline in our ways and form too - reconnected to the Light and Love we are and always have been infinitely part of.

Consider the shape of the heart - two sides come together, each one a part of the whole - male/female, dark/light, Lemuria/Andromeda, Earth/Sky, yin/yang. The Earth is our green/blue planet - the heart itself, an expression of divine love from Source. It is our destiny to harmonise, to bring together, to reconcile through the divine expression of our intuitive feelings and become the Emerald of the Manifest divine heart.

Mary Magdelene is an important Soul energy of Lemuria, a carrier of the purest divine feminine love - Her wisdom was lost in transcription and corruption. and the words of Master Yeshua, now known as Sananda, being her partner. As the Divine Feminine timeline is now healing and restoring we welcome their Truth and their presence as a Divine key of integration as we heal and re-member through the ascension energies.

After the devastation - the plants and crystals became the carriers of Her Light and Love so that the Beings in their Earth bodies could nourish themselves, body and soul to continue their journey path back to the Heart - the Source of Light and Love. Crystals would form a large part of this and yet they allowed themselves to be altered too by being reprogrammed, stripped of their Light Seed. But we continue onwards, the Light and Love of the world needs to be remembered and we see it reflected in true Nature. In the crystals and plants that are safe in the ground and with those who revere their energy and power. In the plants that grow wild and free or are used with Love to make medicine. For only Love is real - only Love will work - only Love will continue into the golden age - this is the way - this is our destiny.'

Rhosalaria - 4th June 2017

The Lemurians speak about Love :-

'In Lemurian times and now in higher dimensions, it was all about Mother Earth. We protected her, we loved, cared for and nurtured her and she knew our love and she gave back Her love through all Her fertile beauty - all we could see touch, feel, smell, was a manifestation of Her love and gratitude. We were inextricably linked between our Galactic families and the energies of love and the immense power of Mother Earth.

There was and still is no time - as we had no need to measure it. As you remember Lemuria, or connect to your starseed, you are living those lives now - for you are a multidimensional Being of Love.'

Please pause here to feel the reality of this Truth now.

Love and care, purest thought in alignment with Source were and still are the mediums for manifestation and so it is today although many of you have lost this gift of knowledge. This is not to say that any of you cannot re-member. As we mentioned before, we had only but to think and feel with our hearts and our desire would manifest into Being.

You must realise and understand that because you are of Love that this Love is the greatest power you truly have. (They Laugh) . . . it really is that simple. Through eons you have complicated everything and brought the absence of love . . . fear and greed . . . as a tool for manifestation . . .and you have felt the most terrible repercussions of this in slavery and oppression of your true nature.

Feeling and sensing is everything - your soul, your body, your beauty - all that you are is a divine manifestation of LOVE. We know, yes, there is so much pain, so much pain. But we are holding you in LOVE and we are finding Beings like you that are part of our Light family to radiate Love in all ways you can in order to rebalance and heal the sadness and degradation and suffering now on Earth Heart.

Why are we doing this? Simply because this is our mission, this is what we have agreed to do so long ago but the process was intercepted by others, beings that did not share the same Love for Earth and we had to find another way and be patient. Patiently radiating our Light through the dark filters and forces that surrounded Earth/Heart.

You are here to help and assist us in our transmissions of Light and Love to heal Earth/Heart so that she may be restored. You have already been doing this and we will help you more and direct you to where you are needed. Do not allow ego to come in - (laughter). There is no ego - that is, spiritually, it is as it is - pure and Light and perfect. The humanity in you will al-

ways believe you are not good enough or are too good! Do not be fearful. The soul pieces of your existence on the timeline are now being restored as One. We can help others to restore their Souls too through light, healing, communication, crystals, grids, sound. Listen to our instruction.

It is true that some Beings may not ascend into the Golden Age of New Earth. These blessed souls have agreed to remain in within the density of the 3rd dimension for this time. Ascension as you call it is not easy - and many will fall away from the pathway, abort the mission - you already know this is true. The resistance of humankind has been programmed and written into the DNA code as free will - choice but the more Light and Love we can transmit through our Crystal Soul Priestesses, Soul and Light Workers, those who remember their mission, the more we can correct the imbalances within the human being and a way shall be made good for RNA/DNA to be read once more in the full glory of its Light.

~ They are Sounding/singing in celebration.~

You know, you have experienced many healing pathways in this lifetime and your Soul's journey and you have met many powerful Beings - they have been your teachers and please know that you are a teacher too. Learning is teaching and teaching is learning. All this has brought you into this time - this moment of utter presence in the Light so you can remember and in your awakening begin a new pathway of illumination. There is no great secret - it is all simply LOVE!

Forgiveness on the pathway to remembering is key. How can love be given a chance to fully manifest if there is no forgiveness of Oneself, no forgiveness of others? No forgiveness of the Soul? Realise that in essence forgiveness is everything because in the Light of Love there can be nothing that could never be forgiven! You see how simple it is.

We want you to strip it back to its simplicity - LOVE AND KINDNESS - that is all. The crystals are divine manifestations of Light and Love and that, you have already stated. In this way they speak for themselves. Love is all.

Within the dynamics of Soul Mediumship we understand that when RNA is in alignment, the DNA of the Soul is able to read it correctly. RNA is constantly in rejuvenation from a Soul perspective. The fact is that hue-man 'conditioning' has led us to believe that we are separate from Source and we have exacerbated that feeling of separation and abandonment in the structure of our societies, our environment, by eating processed foods and by living in fear. Consistent alignment with Source Love enables our RNA to be complete and to carry the Light through our DNA correctly revealing our true Soul Essence, our Soul's Blueprint. When all twelve strands of DNA are connected within the body cells we have more connectedness and alignment to Source and to the RNA or Soul essence blueprint of who we truly are. Thus we remember our mission here and all that we are within our soul wisdom.

THE HEALING NATURE OF LIGHT

Channel continues:

Up to now you have looked at healing as a journey through what you call shadow working. Yes, the pain and fear needs to be recognised, acknowledged at least, felt and understood but we want to tell you that this kind of work is no longer necessary, for healing can happen in an instant - spontaneously, through the most powerful total transmission of Light in alignment and crystalline resonance. Is it helpful to know why you suffer collectively? Why there is pain? No. In order for you to begin rapid ascension and conscious remembering you must look to the Light and its healing transmission. All pain will be cleared - all suffering will be released - since your destiny and birth right is pure LOVE. Yes, you may from time to time sense and acknowledge a disharmonious resonance in your energy field and release it quickly just as soon as you know of its presence there. Using the power of thought and the power of crystalline resonance. You are coming into the time of 'instant manifestation' now. We wish to say that there is no need to suffer or to dwell on pain. In this time of rapid transformation, what you focus upon becomes your reality. Please focus upon Bliss and Love.

~ Here channel reminds me and speaks of a personal memory to illustrate this theory a little.~

Remember once how you felt so sad and despairing - a temporary disconnect from the Light and then you happened upon and encountered the wonderful Light of the crystal you call apophylite. You had only to look at it, not even touching, just drawing in the shape and the Light of its presence with your eyes. You experienced a healing vibration which at once uplifted your feelings and enabled you to move onwards with renewed joy in your heart. Your soul drew this healing resonance towards you.

Much Laughter ~

This explains why so often there are no words to explain these energies and feelings that you encounter through vibrational healing and crystalline energies. The words you currently use are heavy and encumbered with all kinds of misunderstandings, restrictions, assumption and 3rd dimensional frequencies. These words which carry 3rd dimensional vibrations hold you and anchor you down. When you begin to remember the Languages of Light that are carried through crystals, colours and sacred numbers, the language you spoke in Lemuria, this will begin to speed up your full RNA rejuvenation to help you reconnect your DNA and your ascension will be easier - 'Lighter' - Many of you are opening up to these languages now. (much Laughter.)

You have been weighted down for so long now - let go, come into the Light. We welcome you now and applaud the pure Light and Love of your Soul. For your crystalline nature is part of us and our ascended connection - we are all One - we are all linked together.

Huemankind must not focus on fear at this time on your journey. This is an immense test but vitally important for you all. Yes, darkness exists, but only in the perception of no Light, darkness serves the Light, for without dark you would not perceive the Light. Yes there is fear but by giving attention to that vibration you lower your frequency. Believe us now - change can happen, change is happening now - healing can happen instantly through a total disconnect from the lower frequencies of fear. Fear perpetuated in your 3rd dimensional language, symbolisms and media which perpetuates this vibration. Fear - know that it is NOT your resonance - none of you - it is created through your disconnection from the Light.

You seek to release yourselves from fear through alcohol and drugs - these temporary fixes will keep you trapped in a lower frequency.

The resonance of sacred plant medicines and crystals will elevate you towards your permanent reconnection to Light and Love. We Love You. <3

A note here on Light Language: Our modern languages are all descended from Light language. Light language is often conveyed through the visual forms of colour and geometry but Light language itself comes from Lemuria. The languages of Aramaic, Hebrew and Sanskrit are the closest to that original language and so they have been changed and transformed by various civilisations and dimensions. Many people have been channelling language and writings in their own remembrance of the Lemurian Soul. I began channelling such light language when this journey within the Lemurian Remembering began. Light language often comes through to us in channel during crystalline transmissions with sacred crystal healing mandalas. Some of the languages spoken by the Native Americans are also very similar to Light Language. All languages carries a transmission of Light for they stem from the one Light Language of Love ultimately - many languages such as the Welsh language can sound like a song when spoken and listened to. These languages are ancient and have their roots in the stars.

It really is so important that we awaken to the magic and dream of the natural wonders of our Earth now. There is no illness or imbalance that cannot be corrected by the healing magic of the plant kingdom or that of the crystalline kingdom. We indeed live in an Earthly paradise. We are currently shifting out of the dualistic 3/4th dimensional reality into 5th dimensional joy. Fear arises out of the duality within that is associated with fear and conditioned memories and behaviours.

Since we have lived so long in fear it's not surprising that our dualistic nature is the very thing that we are battling against during this time - a tough process indeed. The lower frequencies and conditionings of fear vs. the blissful love vibration that is our Truth.

During my plant communication with Wheatgrass, I was given a vision of a beautiful green mirror which could be accessed by climbing a wall. The mirror could be viewed from the top of the wall and I was able to see into a vast and beautiful garden of Eden. The experience filled my heart with joy. I knew that this was the true reality for us as hueman beings, our potential, our reality free from the chains of fear, illness and conditioning. Channel continues :

Remember the visioning and re-connective experience that occurred when you took into your body the rich and powerful properties of chlorophyll via wheatgrass juice. You at once felt the energetic movements in your solar plexus, the urge to vomit - nausea - a release of fear stored in your physical body. You were then called to sit on the bare Earth - where you were connected at once to Her negative charge - the grounding which allowed your senses to open like a great vessel to understand and know what you had seen and experienced through your heart/3rd eye connection. The feeling intelligence. The resonant vibrations of the plant kingdom are as you know an immense gift on Earth/Heart. It is true to say that the plant kingdom has been huemanity's primary and most obviously powerful and prolific healer through time. As you reconnect to the greater energy of your Souls, and the false soul ego diminishes, this will become yet more evident and their power will be central to your sphere of consciousness.

As crystal is a manifestation of Love and Light - so too are the plants since most cannot exist without Light, the lifeblood within them in the form of chlorophyll is the breathe of life - their very existence is Love. Plants and crystals are the primary sentient beings on Earth/Heart. For they were here always to serve huemanity for natural medicine and wellbeing.

The perception of darkness exists upon Earth only to serve as a mirror for you to see the Light. Once you have fully chosen the path of crystalline ascension there will be no need for this mirror. As you move into the Light and connect to your Light Bodies fully, darkness will cease to have power over any of you because it is not real. It is merely the shadow. Darkness serves the Light - if there were no dark, you could not see the Light! This is why it is so important that when there is a disaster - an act of hatred and violence in your world you must send and transmit Light and Love instead of fear and hatred - in this way the fear and darkness cannot conquer - the darkness will be *overcome in the hearts of all beings. It is only by connection with the dark forces that these atrocities will continue and be perpetuated on and on. Transmit compassion, know that Divine Mother Source holds you all in Love and Light always, always, always. <3*

This last paragraph is so profoundly relevant in our current global situation as the battle for the Light truly plays out. It is all too easy to engage in fear and so perpetuate the narrative governed so long by forces of darkness. Remember that dark is just an absorption of Light that cannot be seen. The frequencies of Light and Love are omnipresent even in the darkest times where shocks are rippling through our daily realities. All that is playing out at this time serves the Light ultimately. For the 3D narrative has been co-created to serve as a catalyst for our awakening. Each shock wave is an interruption to our conditioned fear and an opportunity to awaken the awareness of our own deep consciousness and divine integration.

SACRED GEOMETRY

Sacred Geometry exists within all living things. Each living being upon the Earth has a pattern of its own. Look at the petals of a rose or any flower and see how they form a pattern of geometric uniformity from the outside to the centre. See how the central seeds of a sunflower spiral inwards. Look at the patterns of a leaf or count the petals of a daisy see and know that the formation and number are all relevant as a source to the energy it is radiating. Our whole Being is a network of electrical photonic impulses of electrical energy which forms a grid work within the body and throughout the subtle bodies. Our Soul is the carrier of this network of energy and the blueprint of consciousness for who we are in all lifetimes.

As a Crystal Soul Priestess and healer you will remember that the sacred geometrical patterns created on and around the body for healing integration is very profound. Sacred geometry is key to understanding the nature of Crystal Soul Healing. Channel Continues from the Lemurian elders :

On the subject of Sacred geometry - You understand that everything in creation has its own vibrational resonance. This resonance is unique in itself but there are patterns which naturally invoke the power of numbers. These patterns create a regular pulse of energy, a regular or structured vibration which encourages entrainment. In this way the vibration of everything can be changed and altered. Animals, plants, people and the Earth and Cosmos too. In this way, all healing change takes place - the nature of transformation - the nature of Source, the Divine Creatress who changes everything - the only certainty is that all life changes and moves in cycles. As is the nature of your Soul, moving in cycles multi-dimensionally. Like the spirals of the rose and the sunflower.

This too is the principle of micro and macrocosm - because through entrainment and resonant vibration everything changes from the inside out from the smallest cell to the largest planet in your galaxy to the remotest star. It is the law of cause and effect. When you change on the inside, your thoughts/feelings - you will manifest a resonant match on the outside of your being. This is how, beautiful beings of love, you create and co-create your own reality, from moment to moment.

Everything in the cosmos vibrates with energy. And because innately you are crystalline in nature you will respond to the crystalline nature of sacred geometric patterning in all ways. This is of course principally how crystals make whole/heal. In other words your own crystalline patterning will come into resonance with the inner crystal geometric patterning to create wellbeing through the principles of entrainment and quantum resonance. When you receive a healing integration through crystal energies you are becoming the crystal, you are One with the crystals that are emanating their energies through you.

The Art of Manifestation

Within the quantum field of consciousness we are constantly changing everything around us from within to the furthest star through our thoughts and our actions. Whether we create/co-create something beautiful or not depends on the resonant frequency of the energy within that initiated it.

Put simply, we are creators of reality. This is why the principle of Love is so important to this planet Earth. We come from love and as the hue-man hybrids we are, it is our mission to restore Love on Earth and help realign the Cosmos to the frequency of Love. Divine Mother Creatress is Love - we are all a holographic expression of Her. We are not separate from Her, we are an expansive part of Her.

Whence our energy is resonating at the frequency of Love - whatever we think to create or do will carry that resonant energy with it. We then feel/sense the desire of that creation or thought and so in turn we manifest change through our right action, or conscious action of Love.

It is said that the Universe, or Creation began with a sound but before that sound came the Desire, the energy of Love from the heart of our Divine Mother. All form originates from desire and all beings within the Cosmos have the power to create in the same way. Thought comes from the Desire within the heart, the sensing and feeling from the heart. When the Desire comes into alignment with the frequencies of our Conscious Action - so shall it be made manifest.

Naturally, if our frequency is hatred, evil or fear so the change will be made to manifest something that is not of the frequency of love. The opposite occurs, yet change is made. Like the ripples of a pool of water when a stone is dropped into it - change happens from the inside of you to the farthest star of the Cosmos.

How powerful are we as hueman beings?

And yet, now is just the beginning. As we move into co-creating New Earth together and move into the Golden Age on Earth, we shall use these principles of cause and effect to create. We live in a reflective Universe where we attract the vibrational frequency that is a match to our own.

~

And of course you know also that the energy vibra-

tion that is created through symbols is also powerful because it works too through sacred number and resonant patterning. Some of these symbols you have called Light Codes. Some of these symbols have been channelled through us and others to help you come into the love and wholeness of pure Light. Some are used in healing. Many symbols have come to be seen as part of daily life in your time - but know that there is a subliminal message transmitted via all shapes and all symbolisms. Symbols have also been used as part of the tools to dull your DNA and your remembering - be aware of this and look around at what you see. How do symbols make you feel? Comfortable? Fearful? Anxious? Angry? Harmonious or Empowered?

Throughout the past 26,000 years of darkness on our planet Earth/Heart we have become conditioned by many symbols such as the cross, the pentagram, the reverse pentagram or cross, the swastika. These are all symbols that by conditioned programming, or re-programming carry a certain energy resonance by intention. These symbols have been altered intentionally to carry a different resonance to the ones they may originally have held.

The swastika is an ancient symbol for the Sun. Symbolic of the Goddess Bridget and the returning of the Sun's Light. The pentacle is a symbol of Venus, of Goddess and of Love. Adopted by the Wiccan movement to represent the Goddess and magic, some may view it now as a symbol of witchcraft and fear. The cross also has a heavy bearing on some Souls. The cross may have been drawn upon your third eye as a baby during christening and rather than being the holy symbol of Jesus upon the cross and his sacrifice as the saviour of huemanity, it is a closing down of the third eye and the pineal gland which is our innate connection to the Light of Divine Mother Creatress or Source God.

When the restructuring of hue-man DNA took place in the times of Atlantis, the great gifts of being able to transmit love and light through eye contact was abused. This is why Atlantis fell. There were many distortions of the original gifts of healing and the power of love that had been given to the Beings of Earth.

The eyes are the windows of the Soul. When we connect to someone through eye contact and complete love and trust, we are able to see directly into the Soul. We may see back through the timelines of their Soul and event sense the purity and beauty of the essence of their Soul. This is the blueprint of the Soul. Feel how powerful this is - and also how it may be abused as surely it has been in the past and during the times before the final fall of Atlantis.

In the 'modern' age of television, advertising, social media, phones, screens etc - we are being fed information, programming and conditioning through what we see. Literally we are being brainwashed and indoctrinated. Some of this information may be good, however much more of it is free from being in the best interests of the ascension process of hue-manity.

How does this happen? Again it is the power of desire, followed by energy frequency, feeling and conscious action. Channel continues:

This is why, you understand, it is so important now for you to be reconnected to your own personal Light Body, to become crystalline. And we shall help you through crystalline patterning and transmission. Becoming whole means you are reconnected to the fullness of your Souls blueprint and strong enough to override any unpleasant vibrations in the form of symbols or other energies that shall hinder your Soul's ascension. This is the nature of platonic solids and Fibonacci spiralling. You will be familiar with the shape of the merkabah, the star of David, cubes and other such shapes. All have meaning in their design, they are all sacred symbols of integration and movement into a state of crystalline wholeness and connection to Source.

Go outside, take a look at the plants and flowers - what do you see in for instance, the shapes of the leaves? the way the petals form on a flower - look for the geometric patterning - it is all there.

You are now becoming more aware, as the body becomes Lighter, as you become more connected to your Light body through the ascension energies and the ac-

tivation of the Light Codes within you, Sacred Geometry allows you to travel easily through the multi-dimensions of the Soul. You shall be able to connect with the greater part of yourself extremely fluidly. In fact this is also the way that you shall be able to bi-locate, through Sacred Geometric Patterning. You have, as hue-man beings always known innately the power of such, hence this is why you have built such patterning into all your sacred buildings, such as churches, cathedrals and the ancient stone megaliths that stand upon the land as power points of the Earth's meridians like acupuncture needles drawing energy down from the cosmos and creating a place of sacred power and Light. These places are portals.

The knowledge and power of sacred geometry is written into our DNA. We remember and understand how powerful it is when we enter into a church or cathedral and we feel the resonance. Even more powerful are the stone megaliths that stand on the Earth. The ancient stone circles, many of which are incomplete in this age. Sadly as the stones became buried in the Earth or dismantled and taken away to build dwellings over the hundreds of years past, some of the energies were lessened in these sacred sites. However, through the conscious presence of people creating ceremony and placing crystals in the ground at these sacred sites, the energies of the circles are once again being restored to their original vibrancy. You can feel this when you visit any stone circles or megalith stones and even the burial chambers of our ancestors.

In Egypt, the pyramids were ravaged of their contents and stones removed too. However their original vibrant resonance still remains. The same is true all over the Earth, where the Ancient people co-created with the Beings of the stars, creating the sacred geometrical sites and remembering their original mission here. These sacred sites are a means of communication with the star beings, the originators of Earth/Heart from whom we are star seeded.

Sacred Geometry in Crystal Healing

The use of sacred geometry in Crystal Healing is extremely powerful. When we place a certain number of the same type of crystal in the energy field of the body, they will form a grid work or net of energy over and around the body. The number of crystals used will create a particular resonant frequency. Number holds power.

The Star of David grid is very often used for balance and centring. This formation is powerful as it resonates with the energy frequencies of the Merkabah. The Star of David uses two interlocking triangles over the whole body. Therefore it invokes the power of 6 - Love on Earth. Try creating this pattern using rose quartz crystals around yourself. Stay in this grid for 20 minutes. Then place an additional rose quartz crystal on your heart or your sacral chakra - how does this change the feel of the grid for you? Now the number has changed to 7. Seven is the number of mysticism, spiritual mystery and challenge. Does this grid help you to feel more trust? More openness?

An even number of crystals in a grid will create a sense of stability and balance. An uneven number creates a sense of movement and flow.

We are beings in a hueman body with the potential for 12 strands of DNA to be re-connected throughout our cellular makeup. As Lemurian Soul Beings we are 12 stranded and akin to the Angelic realms. We are able to fully read the beautiful RNA or Blueprint of our Soul's essence and thus the fullness of our consciousness can be expressed outwards through the highest frequencies of our crystalline form and awareness.

Using a grid of 12 crystals is extremely powerful and takes us out and beyond the normal realms of our perception. We are connected to our Light Body and may travel multi-dimensionally through an extended awareness of consciousness.

Many years ago when the series of tsunamis hit the coastlines of Thailand and then Sri Lanka and so many poor souls drowned, the frequencies and ripples of grief and loss were profoundly felt within the waters and oceans that connect us around our Earth. An energy trace of grief was tangible to all sensitive Beings and the energy was carried through the waters.

Without being aware of what had happened, I had created a grid of six rose quartz and six carnelians around me, therefore creating a vessel of 12 crystals. My intention was to connect to the Love of Mother Earth and feel Her resonance and wisdom. Far from being a pleasant experience I was plunged into waves of grief and sadness. A couple of hours later I heard about the devastation the tsunamis had caused and how so many had died. I realised that this was the energy I had tapped into through my crystalline grid. My conscious desire was to connect to the energies of Mother Earth and in so doing, at that point in time, I felt the overwhelming feelings of grief that was present in the moment. I understood later that this experience was to teach me how our conscious desire and sacred geometry links up and assists us in our greater conscious feeling abilities. Our ability to move our consciousness through the merkabah, the vehicle of the Light Body.

We have for so long been accustomed to living within a third dimensional reality, dimming our own magnificent divine light. Even though we innately know that there is so much more to see, feel and sense, we still find it hard to accept that the Soul's greater and expansive nature means we are infinitely able to connect to the much greater

Light of our own Truth and Wisdom.

The Twelve Layers of the Aura

Our energy field extends far beyond the usual four layers that many healers consciously work with. The first four being the etheric layer (energetically connected to the physical body), the emotional body, the mental body and the astral or spiritual body. Our energy field also contains the Etheric Template layer, the Celestial layer and Ketheric Template, the Transitional Body, the Soul Body, The Integrative body, The Eternal Soul body, The Divine Mind body.

The Emotional and mental layers of the Aura are effectively storage space for blockages within this lifetime. Trauma inherent in the Soul's energy is present within these layers and is readily accessible for clearing. In Crystal Healing practice we work upon these layers frequently. We may feel immensely virtuous for doing so for there is much work to be done here in clearing the blockages created by trauma which then prevents the resonation of the energy block to become manifest as dis-ease within the physical body.

The greater work or understanding for these energetic blockages can be cleared in the outer layers and by using Soul Healing through exploring the Akashic records and in the form of healing Light Rays and Light Codes.

The frequencies caused by trauma create blocks

and must be cleared in this lifetime so that the Soul may fully integrate within its true divine essence. This is the healing nature of the ascension energies.

The fifth body of the Aura - The Etheric Template - contains a blueprint of the physical body, rather like the negative of a photograph. When dis-ease in the physical body exists, much work is needed on this template layer. The Etheric Template layer is connected to the throat chakra and is therefore also strongly resonant with our ability to be ourselves, act upon and express our Truth. This layer vibrates with a pale blue resonance. It is within this layer that using sound and crystals can be the most effective for healing. This layer exists some 1 to 1½ feet away from the physical body.

The sixth layer of the aura - The Celestial Body - extends 2 to 2½ feet away from the physical body. It is within this layer that we can experience spiritual ecstasy. We can reach spiritual ecstasy through meditation and by accessing and working with our Light Body. Spiritual ecstasy is obtained when our heart is open and the third eye is fully linked to the heart, creating a channel for Divine Communication with the Angelic realms and emotional intelligence. This heart/mind connection is essential in obtaining enlightenment/bliss. In this layer we are fully open to the higher divine energy and allowing it to flow directly into the heart. We can feel the love for humanity and all life on Earth and throughout the Cosmos. Through this layer we are open to all consciousness. The colour associated with this layer may be a pearlescent white.

The seventh layer of the aura - The Ketheric Template or Causal Body - extends 3 to 3½ feet away from the physical body. This layer is about a quarter to half an inch thick and vibrates at a very high frequency. The layer contains the energy that flows up and down the central column of the body carrying cosmic and earth energies which nourishes the entire body. This golden cosmic energy powers the whole of the subtle bodies, connecting chakras and auric layers together in their network of Light. Within this layer we perceive that we are infinitely connected to Source and may sense the crystalline nature of our Being and the Angelic Wings of the crystalline Light Body.

The eighth layer of the aura - The Transitional Body Layer - This layer is white and is associated with 'no time'. That meaning that time is infinite and the infinity of the Soul is realised through the infinite possibilities of the Soul's potential and connection to the Akashic records in this lifetime. It is connected to the Etheric Star above the crown of the head. We bring more light and activation to this layer when we use the infinity sign in crystal soul healing through the aura.

The ninth layer of the aura - The ninth layer is the Soul Body layer which is related which helps us connect to the Oneness of Divine presence, the sense of who we are as Soul Beings and is linked to the Soul Star. This layer links us to our sense of Divine presence and that which we came here to do. A knowledge of who we are in the now, the One I am present moment and a connection to what we agreed to do and be in this lifetime. It is a bridge between the elements of Divine Order and bliss. This layer is very ethereal, hardly tangible at all in the physical sense and is very finely connected to the Soul star up to eight inches above the head.

The Tenth layer of the Aura - The Integrative Layer - Connected to the Earth star several inches beneath the feet and lying between the physical and etheric layer of the body. This layer exists as a mirror of the Soul. It is this ethereal body which moves between states of being, astral travelling and between the dimensions and dreamtime. Through this layer we are integrating the realities of all time dimensions of the Soul. Who we have been in the past and who we may be in the future according to our Soul's blueprint and essence. Through this layer we make manifest the Soul's essence on Earth. In Crystal Soul healing we are integrating all in the process of grounding through the Earth Star and deeper still.

The Eleventh layer of the Aura - The Eternal Soul Layer - Connected to the eleventh chakra above the head, this is where the Light Body becomes connected through the ascension process. We perceive Light and the Angelic Wings are completely visible.

The Twelfth Layer of the Aura - The Divine Mind Layer - Complete Integration with Divine Source Reality - complete Oneness and connection with all Higher Beings and Divine Mother Source. When this layer is fully open, clear and active it sends shimmering Light in connection to all other layers of the aura and chakras. This is the outer layer of the aura which shimmers with golden light. This level connects to the whole of creation and through this we begin to perceive that we are connected to all that is, we become one with Source.

Within the practice of using selenite crystal at the end of the Crystal Soul Healing session the intention is to create a sense of integration and connection to the Higher Divine Mind and Universal Consciousness - and a preparation for a quantum leap in the expansion of our own consciousness.

With intention, and with the breathe it is possible to extend the auric field of consciousness almost infinitely. However, we must always remember our intention for doing so and the frequency of our field should always be one of the highest Love and Kindness.

THE CRYSTAL SOUL PRIESTESS

THE LEMURIAN ELDERS SPEAK :

The definition of the word Priestess is One who serves Source. One who is the conduit, the channel for Light and Love from our Divine Mother Creatress. As A Crystal Soul Priestess you are a channel for the integration of divine Light and Love on Earth. As we remember the Lemurian Dreamtime, we shall remember that to be a Crystal Soul Priestess in Lemuria was then and is now a great honour of Service. Time is infinite - to be a Crystal Soul Priestess is being in the present moment absoulutely, for from the point of total heart centred Being-ness, we remember. We remember who we are and what we came here to do and be. By being completely centred in body, heart and soul we may integrate our own divinity and are open therefore to the deeper knowing of what it means to fulfil this role of Service, as Priestess, as Healer. The Crystal Soul Priestess acts in Divine Service with Crystal and heals the Soul through the multi-dimensions with and on behalf of the Light. Remember that all that is Crystal and Crystalline is a manifestation of Light and Love from Divine Mother Creatress upon Earth/Heart in-

cluding ourselves.

Our Earth Heart as the Andromedans call it has long been under the dark and heavy influence of Beings who have sought to intervene with the consciousness of human beings on Earth/Heart and to hold us in fear. This has manifested in thousands of our years under the yoke of patriarchy. A word not used loosely and not meant as a detriment or denigration of the nature of Divine Masculine.

Earth/Heart is a body - a living Being created by Divine Source - Creatress, giver, holder of love. She was created as a manifestation of Love and as a hologram of the Love held by Divine Source. We must first and foremost uphold this fact in our heart-minds above all else and absolutely know that everything at this time in your Soul's experience is connected to the absolute essence that is Love on Earth/Heart. This is why you are here, to help restore the frequency of our Mother Earth Heart to one of complete LOVE.

As a Crystal Soul Priestess - you have been called by such divine reverence - the divine nature that resides within you as a holographic resonance of Source itself. Be under no illusion that to be a Priestess of such crystalline nature is one that requires a purity of heart - compassion - diligence - care - dedication. Your heart must be open and not wavering or doubtful. Working with the crystalline Beings of Light is one of complete commitment. You are here for the purpose of assisting Mother Earth, to communicate Her wisdom and Her keys of consciousness through crystalline transmis-

sion and healing to all Her Beings on Earth and into the Cosmos.

Love and forgiveness is key. And this is no easy task in the current realms of 3rd and 4th dimension but this is the process of ascension. To live in the fullness of absolute divine love and service requires a connection to your own Light Body. To feel into the Divine nature of your cells of Light within your Being and to send love into them as a constant daily ritual through meditation, connection to crystal and a diet which is clean and creates harmony within.

Self Love and Self Care

At this time, 2021, the portals of the fifth dimension are fully open. Many beings are moving through the bottleneck of 3rd/4th dimensional realities and integrating into the full expression of the Soul within the fifth dimension. For some, the release from the lower dimensions of reality and slavery will be harder but in the raising of our consciousness and healing integration all will be well according to what is chosen. We are all here as beings of free will. That is what we are given to believe in the lower dimensions. However, we all have our own Soul blueprint and Soul mission and the Soul will always in all ways guide us to where we need to be if we surrender and listen to the guidance within. There are some souls who have not chosen to raise their vibration to a higher frequency and these Souls will remain in a third dimensional reality. Furthermore there are some Souls whose mission was to complete the ascension journey but instead they will also abort the journey. We have the ability to choose always.

If you are reading this, you are most likely to be upon a journey of ascension or choosing to take the pathway of that reality for yourself.

We are collectively part of the rise of the Divine Feminine energy. We are raising our awareness and consciousness and awakening into a blessed time of nurture, compassion and common unity.

It is so important that we remain in the frequency of loving kindness with our physical body. To bring Light into the body through ingesting pure living foods and to maintain hydration is essential. At this time, many hue-man beings are no longer feeling the need to eat flesh. Eating the flesh of another living animal inevitably means we are ingesting fear and death. It is not necessary, for eating a plant-based diet is full of the green living energy that becomes the 'shining green mirror' and entering into the Garden of Eden, the Garden of our heart becomes a reality in practice. Meditation practice and sound baths are important also to nurture the body and keep a clear equilibrium within. Remembering the wheatgrass initiation spoken about earlier, it's a complete necessity to practice a path of purification so that the vibrations we carry and emanate are truly a frequency of Light and Love within. The clearer our body cells, the more easily Light can be absorbed and anchored onto Earth Heart and the easier it is to resonate with the integrated divinity within ourselves. When we are not truly nurturing our bodies, we are creating a greater stagnation of the energetic blocks within that need to be released in order to fully integrate the Divine nature the Soul's energy. Channel continues :

You may come across great resistance in this process for as you purify your physical body, so you will purify all memories held within your cells on all levels, emotional, mental, spiritual that may give rise to the realisation of the alterations to your DNA in the past. It will awaken those memories and dreams filled with fear, loathing, inducing self-loathing, self doubt, judgement and hatred.

Dear Crystal Priestess, you must implicitly know and recognise that these emotions are arising as a result of those times of damage and corruption. Please take heart. For this is what is meant by not delving too deep into the darkness - recognise these feelings, these emotions and draw in the Light and let the fear go into it. Let the Light dissolve the fear. Most importantly you must send Love and Forgiveness to those Beings who altered and corrupted the DNA for they acted from a place of fear themselves. To not forgive is to allow fear, judgement and hatred to continue and persist onwards through the Universe, rippling outwards infinitely. Remember that your Soul is infinite and is Love. The more Love and forgiveness you can send out individually and collectively, the more healing can take place to create a huge wave of Love and harmony throughout the Universe and all Consciousness.

Divine Mother Source allows you to feel into the fear so that you know what must arise from it - LOVE AND HEALING.

Through eons of time, there have been multiple episodes of corruption on Earth/Heart and you may remember through your soul connection to Lemuria, in those last days how such Love was placed into the seed crystals of Light and given to Mother Earth for Her safe keeping until such time that they would be required for Earth Beings to uncover them, and once more begin to connect to their sovereign Being of Light, sending Love and Light out to all Beings in the Cosmos.

This is an essential part of your mission - it is the very core. You are a channel for Light and Love - an immense and humbling honour. There is no room for ego in any form, instruction will flow through you to be followed by right action. There is no collective collaboration other than that which is divinely channelled and given through absolute Love and for Love. There is therefore no hierarchy, actual or imagined. For any such notion of being better or more 'connected' is a part of the dark patriarchal forces we spoke of earlier and an extension of the false light ego. Therefore there is no right, wrong, ego or judgement. You are part of the whole, part of the One in Divine Service of Healing and Integration collectively.

This is the energetic reality we find ourselves in currently. The emergence from duality. The existence within 3rd dimensional individualism and ego into the collective nurturing of 5th dimensional common unity. Heart centred-ness is inclusive not exclusive. It is not concerned with that which nurtures only the individual ego but that which is for the benefit of all within a community reality of Love and Light.

What follows here from the Lemurian Elders is free from being dictatorial but is in essence the resonation of the frequency of Light and Truth that we are evolving to be. Therefore on reading, one may feel somewhat lacking within . . . .this is not the wish of the Lemurians for the key here is to SURRENDER. When we surrender to Love and Light, we more readily and easily embrace the heart centredness that is free from conditioning and fear.

When your heart is pure and you give your devotion utterly in service to the Light and Love of the Divine Mother and transmit this through the Nature of Her crystals of Light there will be no need, thought or intention to deviate from such.

Furthermore, to teach and instruct and initiate others into this devotional healing practice is not one that can be wholly regulated or given credence measured by what you call protocol of the old paradigms - for each individual has their own sense of Heart and Soul Truth. That this must be nurtured and given space to grow is of the utmost priority and importance.

All learning is taken and assimilated into the heart - so the initiate can begin to learn, know and trust that which comes from the heart is what matters and is effectively a conduit for Love and the manifestation of Love on Earth/Heart. Since the times of DNA alteration, you became accustomed to the logic of the left brain hemisphere and the wider peripheral, spiritual cognition of the right brain has become less widely used for many. It is the balance between left and right hemispheres that seeks rebalance and restoration. When the hemispheres are balanced, the third eye and heart open, the channel for higher mind feeling intelligence is open.

Learning and teaching by rote is absolutely not of the heart and comes only from a place of duality, fear and slavery to the old paradigms.

Know that only the devoted initiate will continue their journey of becoming the Crystal Soul Priestess to its fullness. Know and trust in that innate wisdom. Know and feel whether you act from a place of Love or from a place of self appointed authority, fear and ego. What is required is a sense of freedom to flow with wisdom and in-spiration.

THE ELEMENTS AND THE ASCENSION JOURNEY

The Lemurians speak:

The Crystal Beings are a manifestation of Love and Light in physical form upon Earth Heart. They are a manifestation of the love and light within all the molecular elements and minerals created by Divine Mother Creatress as expressed in their geometric and amorphous patterning to specifically emanate and transmit their own individual vibration of Love.

These mineral elements are present throughout the Cosmos and some are present within your physical body also. The vibrations of the Crystal Beings was made dense by those who inhabited Earth within the first Lemurian incarnation and by Divine Mother herself in order for you to see them in physical form.

To hold them, recognise them and admire their beauty has prevailed through your hueman incarnations.

Hence you have, for thousands of years adorned yourselves in the sparkling essence of these Crystal Beings to elevate and enhance your own divine radiance and beauty! We want you to know that the Crystalline Transmissions are of great importance at this time for as you humans raise your consciousness - so the frequency of the Crystal Beings opens to allow more consciousness and Light to flow to you and through you via their energies.

You are waking up - you are re-membering and we applaud you. The Cosmos applauds you!

The geometric shapes and amorphous patterning within crystal creates a variety of energy within the transmissions of Light. There are seven crystalline patterns within Nature created upon Earth/Heart plus amorphous crystal, meaning there is no regular internal/external patterning present. The crystalline formations are trigonal, hexagonal, cubic, tetragonal, monoclinic, triclinic and orthorhombic. Each formation lends a particular energy signature to the transmission of Light from its crystalline form. For example all crystals which appear in cubic form have a similarity in the movement and transmission of their energy.

Therefore when we are creating crystalline mandalas and crystalline transmissions of energy, being aware of some of the inner structural patterns of the crystals used is a key to creating the desired energy frequency. Considering consciously the inner structure of the crystals used creates a more positive, strong radiance of Light transmission for healing and integration.

It's important here to know that all crystalline forms within the Earth essentially originate as a manifestation of Love and Light. The way their energy is transmitted is dependent on their form. Each crystal has an energetic 'movement.' Their colour resonance also lends an energy signature to the energy of the individual crystal being. However, the way in which we translate or assimilate the frequencies of crystals depends upon the energy frequency with which we are currently resonating. This is hence why we are so attracted to certain crystal beings at various times and can readily absorb their healing energy. We come into an energy entrainment with the crystal. We enter into a symbiotic resonance between ourselves and crystal as One Being therefore integrating the divine essence of love and light held within the crystal being. As our energy field is constantly changing, fluctuating and evolving, so our desire or need to work with a particular crystal energy changes too.

As we all become more consciously aware through the ascension process, so we are able to feel, transmit and work with the higher consciousness of Crystal Beings. For each crystal being has so much more information to be revealed as we become ready, open and aware enough to receive it.

ATTUNING TO AND SENSING CRYSTAL ENERGIES

There are so many ways to attune to or sense crystal energy. When we come into contact with crystal an exchange of energy is made. We feel and sense crystal energies readily through the portal of our heart and it is essential that before we attune, we are aligned correctly within our Being - that is, fully grounded through the Earth Star and centred within the heart.

We may simply hold the crystal to our heart and feel/sense what is happening and what is being given to us. Being open through the heart to all we sense, hear, vision, opening to the symbols and words that come to us and also how we are feeling in our own Being whilst attuning to crystal. Through the entrainment of frequencies we sense through feeling. Therefore we shall always remember the energy of that crystal for it leaves a resonant energy frequency within the matrices or energy network of our body and heart.

We also sense crystal energy by surrounding ourselves with a grid of the same crystals. In this case we are sensing personally the healing energy that the crystal is bringing to us. Another person will not experience exactly the same feelings. We are all unique and our energies are unique. Each crystal grid meets us in our energy where we are in the present moment. Energy is fluctuating and changing from moment to moment. A healing grid of rose quartz one week will not feel exactly the same the following. The same is true of all crystal connections. As we attune to crystal more and more we become more open to what we sense and feel.

It is important to note that when we attune to or sense crystal energy that we are not meditating with the crystal. To meditate with crystal is to bring the crystal energy into your meditation session as a focus or by intention to enhance the meditation.

For this reason, to become the Crystal Soul Priestess, it is essential that you know and sense all the crystals in your healing collection. You cannot create a successful healing if you are free from having a clear energetic memory and knowledge of each crystal you are using. We cannot therefore prescribe crystals without tuning into the energies of crystal or the energy frequency of recipient for healing. That said it is always good to trust what you feel, intuit and the deeper knowingness or cognitive memory of your heart and soul.

CHANNELLING THROUGH CRYSTAL

As we become more aware of how Crystal is communicating with us, we may at some point sense that we are opening up to Source energy directly or the energies of some Cosmic or Angelic Being. We may begin to spontaneously channel through messages that are free from being purely the energy of crystal having a dialogue with us but an even greater expansive energy of Light.

Essentially, Crystal is a holographic expression of Source. When we are connecting to a Lemurian seed quartz crystal we are tuning into the energies of Lemuria and we may begin to channel the message of a Lemurian Elder. Remembering that the seed quartzes are amplifiers of the resonant energies that lie within you too. If we channel through Lemurian Quartz, we are often re-membering the essence of Lemuria through our own Soul memories within the Akasha.

I'm reminded of a Crystal Healing class where we sat collectively attuning to Angelite and to our delight collectively experienced an Angelic Being channel through us all. We all received the same message and it was clear that the atonement was not 'just' an atunement but an example of channel through the Angels with Angelites. The message was needed to be heard by us all in that moment and also to teach us that working with crystal truly opens up the connection to the higher divine mind and Source ultimately.

When we are aligned, grounded, centred and connected to Divine Mother Source through Crystal. we may receive Her messages and enter into a Soul Channelling. Giving Soul back to soul through Source and the Heart of the Akasha.

PROGRAMMING AND DEPROGRAM-MING CRYSTAL

The programming that the Lemurians left within each crystal was of Love, Light and remembering. However, because each Soul has choice and free will within the 3rd dimensional realms upon Earth Heart it has been possible to remove the original encoded messages within the crystals and to replace them with something of a lower frequency.

Your computer chips are made from programmed quartz. There have also been attempts to corrupt crystal energies by the Arcons, Dracos and some Annunaki races that have co-habitated Earth/Heart for many years.

This is why dear Crystal Soul Priestess, it is so very important to choose crystal from your heart-centred wisdom and knowing and to keep your heart open and clear. Your heart is your emotional intelligence. This is also the reason why crystal must be kept energetically clean and clear from negative energies which interfere with the optimal functioning and transmission of Light and Love.

It is therefore not within the remit ethically speaking that the Crystal Soul Priestess programs crystal beings for specific functions, but instead chooses the crystal that already resonates with the purpose in mind.

Dedication of a crystal being for a specific purpose is different. If the crystal is willing to be used for healing, for meditation, for planetary and cosmic healing or as a personal magical amulet then it can be dedicated energetically as such in a prayerful intention or ritual.

Channel continues:

As you become more consciously aware there will eventually be no requirement for the Crystal Beings to be so readily available to you in their physical form - they will become more ethereal in their nature. As you become familiar with crystal energies you will be able to bring their energy frequencies into being by intention alone. This is part of the skills remembered in becoming the Crystal Soul Priestess.

Some Crystal Beings such as those you name celestite and selenite are already only partly tangible as an energy form in your 3rd/4th dimensional existence. Their greater resonance exists as a part of the multi-

dimensional realities and they choose to be of a very ethereal nature to you at this time.

Some Crystal Beings are particularly connected to the Beings in other higher dimensions such as the Amethyst Collective - who are spiritual guardians and wish to bring peace to huemanity during the ascension process in the fourth and fifth dimensions. Angelite is particularly of course connected to the Angelic Beings and Guardians that hold Light around and upon Earth/Heart. Azeztulite was a crystal being manifestation through connection held with the Azez Beings who placed their immense knowledge, wisdom and Love for Earth stored within this particular crystalline quartz structure. Genuine azeztulite is now non-existent almost in this 3rd dimension. There are so many others - apophylite, danburite, kunzite, aquamarine/morganite . . .

There is though none so wonderful and praised as Rose Quartz. For She is the purest essence of Divine Mother Earth and a guardian and upholder of the Light in your 3rd/4th dimension. She is a bridge, a conduit to other existences and dimensions of Light, holding you safe whilst you travel and expand in your ascension. She holds you safe where you are now, bringing comfort and the purest essence of Love and through Her essence She is a portal, a connection to Divine Mother Creatress - Source of Love.

Each home, work place and public places too should be adorned with the essence and vibration of Rose as she is the complete manifestation of Love on Earth in crystalline form. Rose quartz is a comforter - and should be given to every newborn human Soul in order to welcome their vibratory senses to that of our Earth/ Heart Mother.

Upon your ascension journey to full reconnection with your Light Body the very simple, generous, uncomplicated and unconditional nature of quartz may feel too heavy for you. Many have come to this already - regarding rose quartz as quite heavy and dense in energy and to be utilised to assist connection to Mother Earth through the Earth Star beneath the feet rather than the heart chakra. This grounding energy being more appropriate than for the heart. This is the changing nature of working with the Crystal Beings - there is always change, evolution into higher consciousness and much more to learn and be aware of.

As you move into higher dimensions of consciousness and the Crystal Beings become ethereal energies it will be possible and necessary to call upon these energies via thought and intention for your healing and transmissions. This is a very necessary skill of the Crystal Priestess and one that is extremely important. Many of you have already experienced this by 'accident' so to speak when you have experienced no physical presence or availability of certain crystals during your healings. This is of course why it is of the utmost importance that you are able to know a crystal energy by its feeling - a connection to it through your emotional/sensing frequency. Your heart connection is, you remember the collector and storehouse for all feel-

ing vibratory resonances and it is your feeling heart centre that recalls such vibration and shall manifest it into being through heart-mind intelligence.

Try this for a moment :

Whatever the crystal energy that calls to you at this time, allow yourself a few moments to sit and feel the vibration of that energy just by recalling its frequency within your heart and mind. Feel the energy resonance within your physical body.

This is what is known as crystal attunement as written in more detail above. As a Crystal Soul Priestess you hold many crystal energy frequencies as attuned crystal energies within the memory of your body cells. It is your unique sensing perception and memory of each unique crystal energy that is key and important to you. When you come to require a crystal for healing, you shall be able to recall the crystal frequency that you need to use in that moment. This is what is known as 'Ethereal Crystal Healing'.

It is this frequency memory that allows you to choose and transmit the appropriate healing crystalline transmission when it is required within a healing or meditation session.

THE NATURE OF HEALING

What is the true nature of healing? Why is healing so necessary for huemanity at this time? Healing means to make whole. Healing is the process of integrating the divine nature of our Soul within to make us whole. We are Light Beings living in a 3rd and 4th dimensional reality. As we move through and let go of the duality of 3D, we are able to integrate the Divine nature of our Soul within. Through healing we become the Super-humans, homo-luminous, the Angelic hueman being on Earth.

A Channel from the Andromedans continues here.

Your astral body is at present in the 3rd and 4th dimensions, your key connection to Source.

It is at the astral layer and beyond that where there is a direct connection to Source, Divine Mother, an open channel of communication through your heart chakra. The astral layer of the Aura and beyond is what you call the Subtle Bodies. The connection to

Source through the reality and recognition of your Soul Self lies in the Light portal of what you call the higher heart or dolphin chakra, ananda kanda at the location of the thymus. Therein lies the Celestial Tree, the ecstatic joyful blueprint for your ascended journey, the true RNA of the Soul Being you are, beautiful and profound.

It is within the current hue-man conditioning at this time that you feel a longing to return home to Source, you sense this urging through your heartfelt feelings. Source, Divine Mother, God, Goddess is home and you long to be there to be connected. Divine Mother Source wishes to integrate with you also, for She loves you dearly. You are inseparable. You are free from being in separation from Source but a beautiful divine expansion of Source.

Whenever you experience great natural beauty through your open senses, give and receive compassion as an open interaction, re-member your past lives through your soul's essence, experience deep and profound soul healing, you are directly connected to Source for She flows through you constantly as a reminder of who you are in Truth and wholeness. Your heart is a reflection, a mirror of Earth/Heart and Her Love - all that you are. . . .and Earth/Heart is awakening and the Divine Feminine aspect is rising. Now is the time for the return to your Great Divine Mother - an integration.

Since you reside currently in the realms of duality within the 3rd and 4th dimensions, with the resist-

ance, fear and the corruption of your DNA - so Earth/ Heart feels enshrouded with such fear and grief - a separation from Divine Mother Source whom She is part of. Although Gaia as the ascended living embodiment of Divine Mother Source knows that it is Her divine right to be part of the Journey home and that you and all Her Beings are part of this also. It is essential that you care for your emotional body and wellbeing. You see, it is a direct link to Source and to Earth Mother. Your body in its physical/etheric and wholebeing form is a conduit of Love and Light. Your body is the Temple of Love. Holding love, transmitting love and so you shall care for it well. When you feel love and compassion constantly as a wave of energy through your heart - so it flows out and back to Source and to Mother Earth connecting all in a beautiful vibrant iridescent glow of LOVE. This flow of Love is vital for the return and ascension of all Light Beings throughout the Cosmos.

You see LOVE IS SIMPLY ALL.

Take a moment to feel this now.

When your heart is acting as a clear channel, your emotional imbalances shall be healed. Since anything that is not in total entrained resonance with Source will cease to exist as you cease to be resistant in letting go. At present you see and accept your heart chakra as a centre of dark and light, a duality, a bridge between heaven and earth perhaps, but when it is purely a conduit only for Love and Light this duality becomes a gateway of direct and permanent connection between the Cosmos and Source Creatress and the Earth you hold so dear. When you become this channel - you change everything around you as other beings slowly begin to come into resonance with the Love you are channelling. For you are a Being of Bliss! You become a part of the 5th dimension and beyond.

Appreciation within the process of ascension and healing is key. Appreciation of Mother Earth/Heart and your environment, including the physical body Temple which you inhabit. The sensations of your sexuality, ecstatic bliss, creation, procreation, the nature of knowing and feeling happy within your body. These are the feelings of LOVE as they flow through the 1st, 2nd and 3rd chakras. Appreciate the insights you receive from Source and the ability to speak and sing and sound in reverence of Her nature and Love through your upper Chakras.

Open to receive Her Light and your Akasha will open revealing the utmost beauty of your Soul's remembering - connect to your Light Body and allow yourself to flow with love totally - this is complete appreciation. - with divine Blessings.

~

Accessing the Akasha of the Soul within the Universal Heart of Source is a valuable skill in our greater healing and ascension. We are able to access the Akasha from the 3rd/4th dimensional realities purely to access the Soul Blueprint fully and also to recognise and heal trauma which is held as a blockage within the energy of the Soul. In the higher dimensions of our multidimensional Soul nature, we have no reason to access the Akasha since all is One, all is healed and integrated within the Akasha. It is only because we sense ourselves as separate from Source Creatress and have a less enlightened and complete view of who we truly are, that accessing the Akasha is necessary for healing at all. There is no real separation from Source. We shall look at this more.

THE SUBTLE BODIES

Andromedan Channel:

Some view the chakras of the body as powerful inhibitors that keep you enslaved to your 3rd dimensional physical being. This is in part true but only as a notion or idea of fear and darkness inflicted upon you. Do you believe such to be true? When you are circulating Light and Love through your body constantly, you are free! You are free from existing within the seven chakra system but a multi-dimensional system of 12 chakras and 12 stranded DNA.

We wish you to take a few moments now and to visualise this. See your physical body as a body of Light. Open your crown chakra and allow your Soul's Light to come close through your soul star. Allow clear Light to flow freely into you and see it filling up all the spaces within your body and your cells. See now the connection of the Earth Star which connects your body to the Earth beneath your feet. See and feel the Light moving out through your aura as far as it will *go out into the Universe! See your Soul Star opening above your head and feel the golden glow of your Incarnational Star within your hara (between your solar plexus and sacral chakra) - now feel the expansion of Light radiating outwards in your heart chakra. All other chakras are channels for Light and Love passing through them. You are a network of Love and Light. See and feel the power of Love connecting you to Source and Mother Earth. Hold this feeling vision as long as you can, see the Light as a circuit moving down to Earth and back up to Source through your body. You are truly a Being of Light and Love. <3*

Your Light Body is immense and can reach out through the stars to all Beings and all worlds - you are perfectly safe - held by Mother Earth and the Earth Star connection within your body.

~

The Andromedans love the essence of FREEDOM and truly wish to convey that you are a FREE SOVEREIGN BEING and that the process of healing and ascension is for the most part the realisation and recognition that you are FREE. So long has this planet been held as a prison by the Beings of Darkness and we have long perpetuated this narrative. The time to find the Freedom from within yourself is here. This is the essence of the Ascension Process. More on Sovereignty later.

~

Your emotional intelligence is what keeps you con-

nected as a constant life source to Source! Your heart is a receiver and transmitter of Source Love always - even when the physical body has ceased to be strong and the mental body is confused the heart will continue to be a channel - as a Being can still feel - your soul's essence shines and radiates through your heart! Feeling leads to salvation - freedom - the pathway to Source which never ever dies away or ceases to exist and flow.

In your world now and indeed along the timelines or narratives of the Soul there are many woundings. Some which run very deep. There are many ways in which you can address these wounds - counselling, psychotherapy - but purely and simply a strong connection to divine Mother Source is the most nurturing and healing path to heal all deep woundings. For through the channel between heart and Source there is only Love and Light which can clear, calm, soothe, nurture and make whole ultimately. No wonder that the most deeply wounded souls often make the most compassionate healers since so deep, strong and profound is their connection to the heart and love of Source.

Pay close attention to your deep feelings and emotional intelligence at all times, your heartfelt intuition, for it is never wrong. You know in your heart of hearts as you say, that when you make choices that do not resonate with the truth of love held within your heart, particularly those you do in pursuit purely of money or ego, or perhaps through coercion from others, that the heart will lose the innate and ecstatic sense of Joy. Your need for connection to Source sweetness becomes more urgent, and so often then you become entangled in addictions to habits and substances to replace the sense of wholeness and sweetness and joy that is a rite of experience through divine connection.

This is the sadness now profoundly prevalent on Earth/Heart - the disconnection through your heart and feeling channel to Source, and we urge you now, encourage you, to seek out all ways to connect to Source daily in ritual.

Divine Love is all. Simply all, and there is no true Love without it. You know this - feel it now - the sense of joy and love which you sensed perhaps in innocence as a child. Feel into that innocence - simplicity - wonder - there you will find LOVE. Remember how it was when you were a child, the first time you saw the vastness of the ocean, a beautiful bright flower, looked up at the bright blue sky or saw the amazing array of shining stars and as a child, you were in awe of what you saw - this is the innocence that is a direct connection to Source Love. The return to innocence.

There is so much to be learned from our Child self. Our Inner child. When you were a child you were still so intensely connected to Source, you could remember more easily all that you are in your Soul through the multi- dimensional nature of your soul self. You played out some of those lives in what you call 'make-believe'.

In a sense, as you grew to adulthood, you devolved from the wonderful wise, freedom loving child self into the adult who forgot their identity and sovereignty. The essence of love and joy ceased to flow so easily through you. You became more disconnected from Source and could not feel or believe in such Love and innocence, as the energies of the dark prison surrounded you and weighted you down. We urge you now, to take time to play within nature. Nature is already in a higher frequency dimension and fully Light connected. Whence you allow yourself to breathe in the fresh air that is all around you, fill your heart with air, look around at the colours of the natural world, feel your feet upon the Earth - you are once more instantly connected to Source Love.

~

The New Earth grids were complete in the year 2020 and the old Earth is crumbling. Many Souls are now shifting their energies to the New Earth frequency of Love. At this current time, you are shifting through portals of energy marked by your lunar and soular calendars. This process brings much Joy to you and as you become more willing to release the old and that which is attached to the old paradigms, so shall you become more at Peace.

THE MULTI-DIMENSIONAL NATURE OF SOUL

Through the increased awakening of your own divine consciousness and ascension you will become more aware of the multi dimensional world you inhabit. When this awareness increases so much more will begin to make sense! This, together with the release of fear and dependence within your 3D existence shall create an immense sense of immediate elevation and freedom and sovereignty becomes reality to you and so much will open up for you! So much.

Yes! you are free to move through other dimensions - YES! This is how we have been able to visit your planet for millennia - through the power of higher dimensions and consciousness. The drudgery you experience in the 3D world as 'normal' is in fact illusory. So much more is and has been open for you to know and to see for so very long now. You had forgotten much of this through the dark times of corruption. Your soul is fluid - it is Light energy that travels across space and time with no boundaries through consciousness.

In the 3rd dimension you feel longingly that there must be more and that longing overwhelms you. The Truth has always been there and you can just reach out and touch it, feel it, live it. For Divine Mother Source does not want Her children to feel trapped or enslaved. The ascension process and opening to consciousness is the key to freedom. This is what is playing out in your current narrative now in 2021.

Living within the 3rd dimension is a choice that you made for this incarnation in order to learn, heal and integrate and also to be of assistance to those Souls who are also learning and healing. For whence we learn, we are also teaching others.

Within the 3rd dimension lie the energies of broken timelines, trauma and drama which is played out over and over through patterns of behaviour and belief. Also existing within the 3rd dimension is the nature of duality. Duality does not exist in the fifth dimension. As you are now moving through into the fourth dimension you understand this. Understanding the nature of 3rd dimension happens within the fourth. Fourth dimensional reality and understanding is the preparation for the 5th dimension. Experiencing and living in freedom from duality is the reality in 5th dimensions and beyond.

Why does duality exist in the 3rd dimension? Why did you choose to be here? These are questions that can be answered by looking into the multi-dimen-

sional nature of your Soul and by understanding the mission you have here on Earth/Heart at this time. You all have a mission. The mission is essentially an inside job! (laughter) For whence you become aware of the processes you are undertaking to integrate your divine consciousness, your frequency shifts and therefore what you manifest upon the Earth will shift to come into alignment with your Soul's mission.

Duality is that sense of resistance or antagonism between the earthly self and the higher self. The tendencies for resistance to becoming whole, for attachment to trauma, living out the dramas of your earthly ancestors and the traumas of your Soul's story, these stories are like resonant patterns which exist in the emotional pain body often embedded within the sacral chakra - these all exist in the lower frequency earthly self attachment. The higher self is that which is aligned with divine heart and mind, the connection to Source and all that you know you are in Soul infinitely.

In 3rd dimensional reality you are conflicted between the trauma/drama of lower frequency memories and the grace of divine Being. When you can reconcile the two equally - you are centred within the Truth of your Heart. Existing in the true Sovereignty of your Soul. The heart is the portal space which is the direct communicator to Source. In such reconciliation, processing and alignment, there is deep soul healing. 3D attachment to drama/trauma becomes enlightened through the connection and awareness of the higher conscious divine self. Both frequencies become centred within the Beingness of the Heart and through this we may become transformed and journey into the true divinity of our Soul. From this heart space and non attachment to duality - we are trusting of all we are. Grounded in our Earth/Heart body, knowing and trusting our innate wisdom. Recognition of the wounding happens within the heart - it is healed through the heart.

You have come into Being at this time to truly live your Truth and Be Free!

You are entering a time now where to move in and out between the third and fifth dimensions is easier. You may begin to sense that when you are practising healing, experiencing the flow of light and love from Source through your healing sessions, that you sense the elements of freedom and Joy that are the very nature of existence within the 5th dimension.

Upon the Earth plane there have existed stories of visitors to your planet and the abilities to channel messages from beyond the grave and beyond this world of Earth. To know that you, your Soul exists in not one dimension but many, explains quite simply how these communications of love are possible and are indeed happening all the time. In the wholeness of your Being you know this has been the Truth throughout eons of time. Great Shamans, healers, prophets, wisewomen, medicine men through your history have obtained their knowledge through multidimensional communication and travel.

Know that your Soul does not exist at one dimensional level but many simultaneously. This is why vibrational healing is so powerful to your soul and to all the Souls collectively of Earth/Heart now. When vibrational healing takes place in the moment and in connection to Soul, the Soul is made whole. Fragments which you perceive as being broken away in previous life existences in the past and future can be reconnected in order for you to step into the greatness of the Love and Wisdom of your true Soul Essence at this time. You are waking up to the full conscious reality of your Soul in wholeness. When you are healed, aligned with your true Soul's consciousness - ripples of change move outwards across the entire Cosmos to create more integration, more alignment, more healing.

Crystal Soul Priestess, this is your mission. Not just to create wholeness within yourself but also for others and Earth/Heart herself. Many of you have been undertaking this important mission all your lives and we applaud you. We beam our absolute Love, gratitude and appreciation to you now. For as you restore your frequency to LOVE, you restore the frequency within the entire Cosmos. Thankyou.

~

When we approach Crystal and Soul Healing from the point of understanding that all is happening within the present moment, we can create change, alignment and healing throughout all soul incarnations.

The following diagram shows the Soul as a Pyramid of Light. At the apex is the connection to Source, Divine Mother Creatress and a point of infinity. All lifetimes, existences, memories, thoughts, experiences are spiralling simultaneously within the pyramid of Light and at the centre is the infinite heart. The arrow of time or divine presence is that which we align with in the centre. The 'I am' presence. 'I am that, I am.'

This infinite centre point lies within the heart and is the portal to conscious manifestation through and with LOVE. This is, therefore, how we can create our own divine magic upon Earth/Heart.

The Soul is Self. The Soul is what we are and what we have always been and shall be. It is the Light of our Being.

When we speak with awareness the mantra" I am that, I am" - we are saying that 'I am everything in existence that is part of all loving creation. I am One with Divine Source.'

We can change the word 'that' to whatever we wish to affirm we are specifically, but essentially we are part of the all, the One and there is no separation, only a divinely beautiful expansion of Source Creatress. Try the following and spend time repeating over and over. As you do so, feel the change happening in your frequency.

'I am love, I am. I am peace, I am. I am joy, I am. '

Try creating these mantras for yourself. When you say 'I am' you are affirming that you are part of Source and free from separation. You are one and the same in infinite divine presence. Om.

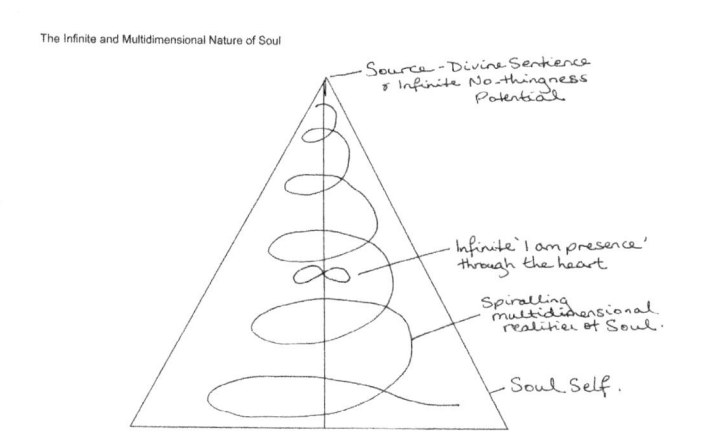

The Infinite and Multidimensional Nature of Soul

- Source - Divine Sentience & Infinite No-thingness Potential
- Infinite 'I am presence' through the heart
- Spiralling multidimensional realities of Soul.
- Soul Self.

Lemurian Channel :

In order for you to be fully aware of and truly feel into your multidimensional existence you must naturally be well and whole in your physical body on Earth. It has long been stated that you cannot be so heavenly to be of no Earthly use. You must be grounded and tuned into Divine Mother Earth and Her negative charge of yin energy for you to experience not only the realms beyond Earth but the other worlds and realities that exist on Earth.

By being safe and grounded within your body you may communicate with and feel the love of the plant world, insect world, bird and animal worlds and of course the world of Crystal.

Please know that by communicating with all life in all the worlds you are strengthening your own vibration on all levels. Know that when you bring the vibration of the plant world and the cosmic healers into your healings that you co-create a greater and powerful wave of cosmic soul healing, not just for the recipient but for you yourself and out into the Cosmos. Since every living manifestation in every worldly existence is a frequency thought of divine Mother and a manifestation of Her Love - multidimensional healing is the ultimate healing there is. A return to Source - a return to Love.

Please use all these tools in your healing, crystals, colour, sound, plants, angelic frequencies and ask for the help of those who are your Galactic Soul Healers. Bring them into your healing mandala Light transmissions, into your sacred Earth places, into your personal healings and self healing too.

Please know in your heart that the greatest healing takes place on a multidimensional level for whenever change is created on an individual level in the Universe, the ripples of healing travel out to effect and touch everything within the Universe. As the Crystal Priestess you facilitate the magical healing touch of Love. This is a gift of great honour and responsibility.

Healing should always be given with humility and not from a point of ego, for you are a channel for Light and Love. Only the highest divine energies from Source may be channelled, if healing can take place at a Soul Level.

The Multidimensional Nature of the Subtle Bodies

The Aura is a part of what you call the subtle bodies As we mentioned, the aura can expand outwards infinitely. There are many layers to the aura and within the auric field you may sense the presence of wings which attach you to the multi-dimensional nature of the Soul self. As your incarnate physical/etheric self becomes lighter and more crystalline, so shall you be more aware of the Merkabah as the vessel for travel of the Light Body. The aura and chakras are a network of Light and energy which is vibrating and changing continuously. They exist not independently but as One Living energy Being, which itself is connected to the living aura of Gaia, Mother Earth, who is Herself connected to all the planets, stars, moons, galaxies in the Universe. We are all One.! You are part of us - we are part of you! So please know, that you are never facilitating or creating a healing in just one place, on one layer, on one chakra, in one dimension - you create a healing for a whole Universe! Healing is LOVE.

RNA/DNA of the Soul

The RNA/DNA nature of the Soul may be hard to understand as a concept since we are so often concerned with such from a physical biological viewpoint. However, as you read I am sure all will become clear. From this point of understanding the nature of the Soul we gain a greater picture of how Light and energy integrates Source with Soul. Channel continues :

The Soul is an auric sphere of Light - the essence of all you are is Light, frequency, vibration and it is held within this beautiful sphere. Energetically, the Soul RNA is an energetic messenger between Source and Soul. RNA is the original single strand essence of the Soul. The Souls blueprint or original essence is stored within the DNA and the encoded messages between Source RNA and stored DNA is the Light Communication between Source and Soul.

Since long ago your DNA was corrupted to be just two stranded, RNA has been unable to completely read the fullness of the Soul's Blueprint. A communication breakdown has occurred between Source and Soul. However, as more Light strands are activated within the DNA, so the messages can be read more easily. RNA is the rejuvenation of the Soul. It can be restored and reprogrammed. Whence it is reprogrammed through AI or biological intervention, the encoded messages between Source and Soul are changed. This may be what is called a detachment of the Soul on a fundamental level.

Within the Soul exist keys to open up the energies of true Desire at the centre of the heart. Desire is free from being the 'I want' ego desire, but the desire which is in alignment with Source and Soul. The Crystal Soul Priestess may bring through many Light Codes to help activate these keys and the keys to healing trauma, therefore alleviating blockages to the full interpretation of the Soul through RNA/DNA expression.

In remembering your True self, in remembering your mission and actively pursuing to fulfil such you are reactivating the fullness of your DNA strands. Light is love, love is life and through the Light which is manifest within Crystal Beings, so much Light can be restored and reactivated within the Being as a whole. Light creates rejuvenation and reconnection to the Souls essence whence the DNA may once more be read and translated efficiently and truthfully by RNA.

Since the Soul is a sphere or aura of Light it is as such manifest within the nature of the physical/etheric Being when we are incarnate in this Earthly form. The nature of the Soul - all that we are, will be and ever have been - the multidimensional self is anchored within what we call the Incarnational Star right at the centre of the physical hara. You may sense this as the seat of wisdom, the centre of knowing - for indeed it is!

The Chakras -

The chakras themselves are multidimensional vortices that are as such anchored into the physical/etheric body, spinning in two directions just as does the Merkabah. The Merkabah is the Light vehicle of your multi-dimensional travel for the Soul. Symbolised in 3D by two interlocked triangles, we see this as the Star of David. A six pointed star, it is also known by you as the symbol for the Heart Chakra. Naturally you understand that whence we are truly resonating from the centre of the heart and our Truth, we are free to travel dimensionally!

The chakras as you may know them seem to be a third dimensional construct. By bringing in more Light and connectedness to Source, change happens - we sense the fluidity of the 5th dimension and the nature of the chakras alters. There shall be more given upon this later.

Let's look at them each here :

The Base chakra -

The base chakra is free from being static although in the 3rd dimension it is symbolised by a square. You may have been used to considering that this square is in fact some kind of anchorage or holding point, a place of rootedness. Indeed in the 3rd dimension it is an anchorage point within the physical body - a centre of all that it is to be within a physical body upon Mother Earth. From a higher frequency perspective it is a gateway to other dimensions of your Soul. The base or root chakra is your anchorage to the physical body in this Earth lifetime, it is that which connects you to your body in physical/etheric form. However, consider the square - being four sided, cubic in nature - it is also a gateway, a portal of connection between this life and others. Opening the sides of the square like doorways and also considering them as mirrors to other dimensions is an interpretation of the multidimensional nature of the base chakra.

There is movement through these doorways. Traditionally you may associate black or dark colours with this chakra. Black is an absorption of the Light - therefore in our knowing - being we are absorbing all Light into our physical body and all Light is held here. Whence Light is brought into the root chakra we may see, feel and know that we can move, dance within this Light, shift between dimensions and realities for through the Light we see the mirrors of the Soul - the doorways between dimensions become fluid and open. We may lose the perception of the static density of the physical being - but this does not necessarily create a sense of being ungrounded if the Soul's Light is properly anchored to the Earth Star beneath the feet. We are free to shift our perspective and to enter other dimensional realities and aspects of our soul self.

Feel free to place crystals which are 'light' upon the Root Chakra, so long as the Client is grounded through the Earth Star, all is well.

The Sacral Chakra - The sacral chakra is an important anchorage for yourselves through the timelines and narratives of the Soul and incarnation. Through the sacral chakra you not only relate to others in the physical sense, you create, recreate, procreate. Through the sacred sexual nature of the sacral chakra you store the energetic memory of e-motion, pain, fear through the timelines of the soul from other existences. As we explained in the section of duality, this pain and fear - trauma is here to be addressed within your Earth life. It is what you have chosen to allow, address and heal. It is a unique and wonderful opportunity for healing. Therefore it is in itself an ecstatic gift. Ecstasy is perceived as a fifth dimensional feeling whence the narratives of the timelines are complete and healed. Through the sacral chakra you sense the gift of bliss - the existence of all that is in Creation - the Light of Source Origin - you may sense that resonation of the first Creation. It is through the Bliss and Ecstasy of the Sacral Chakra that we may co-create over and over bringing through the holographic blueprint of Source within manifest form in many different ways, uniquely resonating love and light as an aspect of our Soul self and Source together. It is creation itself and the dance of creation. This is present within sacred sexual union.

You may work with this energy in shifting fear and pain, creating and recreating a new Soul story - a new 'timeline' and in Soul a part of you is then reborn, recreated through such ecstatic movement. You flow with the deep rivers of ecstasy by facing your fears and moving through them to once again dance with the Light. The Light helps you to regenerate yourselves with the blissful orange glow of Soul and Unity. In your 3rd dimension the sacral chakra is symbolised by a crescent moon - a symbol of divine feminine Cre-

atress. The Creatress of life - the womb of creation, the cauldron within which all things must change and move alchemically transforming. Life, death, rebirth. The element that is associated is of water, through water you leave the energetic memories or traces of all your timelines and the stories of your Soul nature. Here you may be holding trauma and through coming to understand the trauma which is being mirrored or reflected back to you through the sacral chakras in the form of fear which you may or may not know the origin of - you can begin to acknowledge, accept, forgive, release such and begin again. Consider also that in your ritualised world, the waning moon and new moon is symbolised by the crescent - release and renewal, rebirth. Do not hold fear dear beautiful beings - for life is an ecstatic dance - keep moving, shifting, changing!

The Solar Plexus - *is the expression of the inner Sun around which your energy pivots within the third dimension. It is seen as the anchorage point of your own ego/desire/ will within a third dimensional nature - it is the duality between the inner ego/I am and the I am in connection to the central Cosmic Sun - the Light of Divine Source Origin and also the Light at the centre of Mother Earth Heart herself. In the fifth dimensions and beyond you may see through the nature of this duality and flow free. The constant battle of will and desire for all becomes merged in Unity and you realise through the immense Light of Source that Unity between the physical Earthly I am, in connection to the*

Will of Source is the forwards movement for the Soul as it contains therein the absolute Truth of whom you are.

Confusion of identity, of self, over blown ego, lack of self knowing and esteem is identifiable in the third dimension as a disharmony of your solar plexus. Whence you translate the word self as Soul - you then begin to flow with the greater understanding of who you are in Soul. The Soular Plexus. You do not need to hold on to some third dimensional identity which is reflected through culture, fear and static beliefs in the lower chakras. Within the 5th dimensional nature of the Soular Plexus you are One with Source. Symbolised as a equilateral triangle - you understand that the Soular Plexus is also a portal gateway to understanding your Soul Self - who you are - your mission here through the very nature of the Unity of divine masculine, divine feminine and Source. The nature of three in Unity, not the duality of the two.

The Heart Chakra - *much has been stated here already about the heart chakra. The Heart is the centre of your energetic body within third dimensional reality. Symbolised as two interlocked triangles one pointing upwards, the other pointing downwards. They are the connection or centering of the higher self and lower self. All that you are in Soul is seen and communicated through the very centre of the Heart Chakra - the emerald of the Heart. From the feeling perspective all that you are is expressed through the heart. The heart is a direct line of communica-*

tion with Source through the feeling self. In a sense, the Heart represents the RNA messenger energy from Source above into the DNA storage energy within the body incarnate.

Whence we speak of feelings, we do not mean emotions. Feelings are what you sense. Sensing as such with love is the frequency of Love. Emotions are heavier energetic vibrations that are held within the sacral chakra. E-motion, energy in motion. Energy which is shifting, expressing and transforming. Feelings are what you are sensing in the moment of divine Presence with Love.

Consider the Heart - two sides, the divine feminine and the divine masculine in Unity the two sides of your Soul Self divinely expressing outwardly and sensing love and receiving love. The heart is in harmony whence it is open to give and to receive Love. The Divine Love of Source. Breathing in love, breathing out love. Inspiration and expiration - we breathe Source Love. In constant motion. A circle of love and light. The essence of breathing is the essence of our physical and spiritual existence. Your breathe is key, is everything, and is your spiritual connection and your physical connection to life and love. In essence the heart chakra is the Light at the centre of your physical self. Hence the blood is flowing through the body, the breathe is circulated through the body from the physical heart and as such the physical body may be sustained through breathe alone by actively using the power of prana/chi/ki. The prana being the es-

sence of life force within the breathe.

Through your heart you are the sentient being. You are directly the manifestation of love and light upon Earth. This is dear Earthlings why we refer to your planet as Earth/Heart, the same letters re-arranged. Whence you communicate with the Crystal Beings through the entrainment of energy through your open heart you are opening a portal doorway between yourself, the crystal being, Mother Earth and Divine Creatress Source. Through such feeling attunement, Light is transferred through you as photons containing Light Language, which you translate through your own feeling intelligence and the portal or channel between your higher heart and your third eye chakra.

Through the heart as a resonant portal you are in connection with all. All there ever was, all that is. Through the heart you may come to receive through feeling and sensing the resonant energy signatures contained within the Akashic Records.

The higher heart *- is a Light portal within which an understanding of divine consciousness flows as a light frequency of energy. All the bliss and ecstatic resonance of your Soul's expression may be sensed through the Higher Heart. Many people of Earth Heart are closed at this centre as biological intervention and poor connection to Source has closed the feeling nature of this chakra. If this chakra is free from fully radiating Light, then the Heart itself may be depleted and free from being fully open, as the Higher Heart is the centre of understanding all we are sensing through* *the Heart. It is essential that the Higher Heart is re-activated. As a Crystal Priestess, it is essential to keep this portal open and clear just as it is also essential to clear it for those who ask for healing.*

Placing a crystal upon the higher heart and the heart is sometimes needed. Considering these two chakras as one. Often the higher heart will need a lighter crystal to open and clear the portal into the heart itself.

The Throat Chakra *- is a centre for expression in all ways and at all levels of your being. The throat chakra was once a centre of communication via the collective consciousness. The vocalisation or singing of sound which carried the resonance of divine messages and wisdom channelled through the higher chakras from the Galaxies and beyond. The throat chakra is in 5th dimension a portal connecting the higher chakras and the expression of divine communication of love and light through sound resonance. Whence the heart is open, the higher heart is the portal of feeling which transfers the energy of such love and feeling through to the expression of the voice at the throat chakra.*

In Lemuria, we expressed through Light Language which sounded like song. Each being has their own Soul Song which is given at Birth. Just as everything in the Universe has its own sound, each plant, creature, bird, rock and crystal. Sound is the first manifestation beyond the first thought. Whence you connect to your Lemurian vibration, you shall often hear the sounds and the Songs which are the expressions of Light and Love. Sound heals. Sound expressed through the portal of the heart and throat can heal deeply.

Many of the languages in existence have threads of Light language flowing through them. The celtic languages sound like songs when spoken correctly and with gentleness. The hebrew language, sanskrit, and languages of the Hawaiian, aboriginal and native americans all have their roots in such Light language.

During a healing session, your heart is open and connected to the energy of your client. Intuitively you may feel a need to chant or sing some words or just sounds to aid the healing gently. Trust your intuition.

Third Eye/Brow Chakra *- Dear Hue-man Beings your head is a virtual antenna receiving and assimilating all kinds of information from the Cosmos as well as giving out information through conscious connection to the Cosmos! You are such a powerful Being. Within the third eye chakra is the alignment of absolute knowing in Oneness and Unity with Source and the ability for complete understanding of the Universe, Creation and all that Huemanity is within the Cosmos. Your third eye chakra is an anchor point which helps direct Light into the Pineal gland towards the back of your head. This ancient gland is very important. Sadly through the last 100 years it has become deactivated more and more by the poor diets and chemical poisons ingested by many through water supplies, EMF and other negative energies. The Pineal* *is very important to you as a detector of Light. Spiritual Light. Crystals and meditation shall help restore the energies of this gland enhancing the energies of the third eye and the ability to see/intuit more clearly.*

The Crown Chakra - *Receives Light from the Cosmos and brings life force energy to flow through your body. This is the doorway to physical Light connection and to all that is on all levels of your Being. When the Crown chakra is very depleted a sense of 'depression' occurs in the Being as the connection to the Light of the Cosmos is literally cut off. Through the Crown chakra you are able to open up to the higher chakras and gain greater insights and communication with the higher dimensional beings and the essence of Source.*

The Soul Star - *which may be some 6 inches above the head. This chakra or soul anchor point, forms a bridge, a link between the reality you perceive in the physical body and in that reality from the perspective of your body of Light. It is a connection between heaven and earth. At the base of this anchor point is the Golden Crown which contains the Akashic records or the ability to connect to the Akashic Records. Through this you may access the blueprint of your Soul. To reveal who you truly are, who you have been who you shall be. When this anchor point is clear it is possible to access a link to our soul's memory.*

The Stellar Gateway - *exists about a foot above your head. It is a funnel of light that connects you to the divine. When this channel is cleared and open,* *it is possible to connect and communicate with light beings that exist outside of the physical realms. Through this gateway, it can be possible to identify with the divine energy, perceiving the Source as being a part of us. Within the energies of this Gateway you clearly perceive that you are divinely integrated.*

The Causal Chakra - *lies towards the back of the head about four inches along from the crown chakra. In ancient times or when you were beings of more than 2 strands of connected DNA, this chakra would have been part of the brain itself. Realise that this still exists and in reconnecting all 12 strands of DNA the Causal Chakra is fully activated.*

The function of the causal chakra is to allow the true expression of the soul to filter into the physical body from the soul star. The nature and energy of this chakra is Silent Peace. To truly open this chakra one must quieten the mind and allow the heart to fully open thus allowing a clear flow for the soul star energy to come down through the causal chakra and into the physical body. Once this chakra is opened it allows you to feel an immense sense of peace and stillness no matter what else is going on around you. This is extremely valuable in the chaotic times of ascension process you are now experiencing in 2021. Practising meditation and what you call mindfulness truly assists the activation of such Silent Peace.

The Alta Major *lies at the base of the skull at the top of the nape of the neck. This chakra is a place where you hold the memory frequencies or what you* *may call the psychic memory of all that has happened in this lifetime or others. Whence you feel you are under some kind of psychic attack (that is sensing that there are negative thought forms which are directed towards you), this triggers that sense of trauma within the alta major. This gateway is also known as the gateway to the past and as such is a good point to cleanse.* **In a healing session this is not always practically easy to access. If a Client is lying down you may place a crystal very gently just behind the head/nape of the neck.**

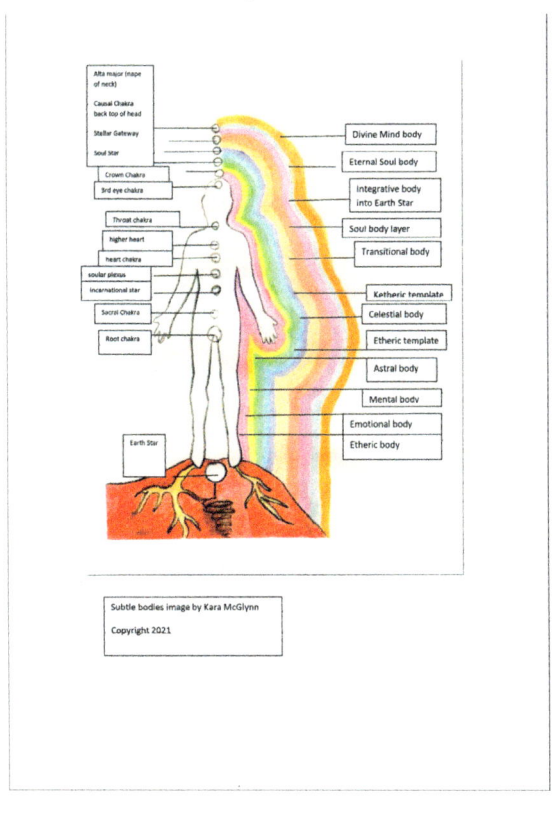

Subtle bodies image by Kara McGlynn
Copyright 2021

THE CRYSTAL ELEMENTS OF LEMURIA

The Lemurians Channel :

In recalling the times of Ancient Lemuria, you remember that the primary element that flowed through your consciousness was water. Water flowed and was/is a connection to your heart and feelings. It is for this reason that the knowledge and codes to Source were placed into the Seed Crystals of quartz. The Quartz beings allowed and resonated with this flow - this is your primary connection to Source - Great Mother.

Other Crystal Beings resonate well to the other four elements - air, fire, earth and the metals. Quartz was left behind in many forms to help you connect back, to travel into other dimensions of your Soul Self and the deep memories of Mother Earth and to be able to understand and assimilate those memories in the Now. That you accept these memories and allow them to be a part of yourself is most important and the nature of quartz is here in this time to help and assist you to do this. Quartz holds and encourages you. Quartz is an energy and a part of Divine Mother that knows your resistances and will help you see, know and understand your emotional and spiritual soul connections, removing and clearing the pathways upon your life's journey here on Earth Heart. Quartz shall connect you to the spiritual beings in the Cosmos and through these frequencies you shall never feel alone but all one with the Cosmos and creation.

Many quartz crystals carry the vibrations of other elements too. Such as smoky quartz which contains the elements of air, earth and water. This of course makes smoky quartz of great value as a healer. The greatest of these being the smoky elestials which embody the energies of the angelic realms.

Whilst the nature of dear blue lace agate - a microcrystalline being who transports you sweetly through the air, skies and clouds to the knowledge of the Ain Sophir where you may listen to, sense and speak to Source directly.

Carnelian connects and speaks to your deep emotions, opening up the narratives of previous lifetimes via all relationship to heal the timeline of the Soul. Carnelian is of Earth and water and fire and wishes you to be most completely present in the current embodiment of your Soul self NOW. Carnelian wishes for you to be ecstatically joyful in all your creations upon this Earth plane.

Green Aventurine, another crystal being that is a micro-crystalline quartz supporting the flow of the emotions - both water, earth and air - allowing you to open to the expansiveness of your heartfelt feelings - to breathe deeply into the expansive spaces of your lungs - to be free and connect to the vast magic of Nature and Mother Earth herself.

Hematite, metal, iron oxide, the elements of connection are air and earth. There are some whom find it hard to connect to the energy of this wonderful crystal being. This is because the nature of hematite is the absolute nature and resonance of the elements found at the centre of our Mother Earth, her heart. The centre, Her heart is that which holds us together, that draws us into the physical, materialisation, the manifestation of our Divine Self on Earth. As multi dimensional Soul Beings, we find it difficult to be so densely physical, to feel the heaviness of Earth, because it is our mission to be seeking the Lightness of Source. However, within hematite lies the most dense manifestation of Source love itself. Hematite will hold you together, will align all your subtle bodies quickly and draw you back into your physical body completely. In this way, hematite is most valuable for physical shock and indeed when our being has become flighty with no sense of direction or focus.

~

You will remember as an incarnate Soul In Lemuria - you were most joyful and ecstatic to be present on Earth/Heart and to enjoy all Her elements. As you originated from the stars it was so wonderful to be in a body, although still so ethereal with all the sensations of Love being manifest all around you to enjoy. The Crystal Beings had formed themselves around these elements so they could be more easily understood - their frequencies read and absorbed readily.

There are so many other crystal beings that offer so much. Each crystalline structure has a particular resonant pattern of frequency, these patterns and frequencies belong to the laws of sacred geometry as we spoke of earlier. These patterns hold sacred power and energy that will appeal to you at varying stages of your Journey. All are filled with Love that wishes to be shared for the highest good and connection to Source.

To share crystal Love is to share, hold and channel the Love of Source

To be Her Crystal Priestess is an honoured Journey. We must learn to face and release our shadows into the Infinite Light of Love and Creation, and not to hold onto shadow as trauma and drama. We act in honour of Her Love always, in healing and as we walk our journey path upon Earth/Heart.

As a Crystal Priestess you have travelled many lifetimes. Your Soul has gathered, fragmented, gathered again many times to bring you into the fullness of the Light of Service you experience in this time NOW.

Hear the calling - perhaps you hear it in the ancient call of the Sea, in the songs you sing or as some distant memory you do not yet understand all this is part of your re-membering and reconnecting.

As you surrender your soul's Light into re-membering and you begin to gather the lost fragments of your Soul, much pain and joy will come to the Light of your Consciousness.

You will remember both pain and joy as a part of the process through which you must experience within the third and fourth dimensions. Thus you shall be better able to raise your vibration further and more rapidly.

It has already been stated that there is no bearing to be had on immersing yourself in shadow. Shadow and pain are part of the Light and so must therefore be seen and dealt with as part of the infinity of Light that is omnipresent. Shadow must be integrated within the Light. In order to assist this release and integration of the healing process - we suggest that a daily Spiritual practice is very important.

Create and re-create with Love and appreciation your own sacred Crystal Altar. Place crystals that speak to your soul's journey in the moment. Use the vibrational healing frequencies of colour with candles and altar cloths. Place any representations of Divinity that call/speak to your Soul and bring the fullness of Love to your heart. Sit with your altar each day - create sound with your voice or bells/singing bowls and align yourself with Earth/Heart and the Stars and your Heart - connect to Divine Mother Source and allow the Light of Her Love to flow through you. Allow the Earthly connections and anchors of your chakras to be filled with Light and to illuminate your soul star, your heart, your incarnational star and Earth Star. Feel fulfilled in the moment with Her Lovelight and feel the Oneness and connection to all - sense the bliss and let it flow. Allow all that lies heavy upon your heart to merge into the Light. As Light flows - open your Soul Star to the Akashic flow and allow the knowledge of your Soul to become manifest and conscious within your Heart and the deepest knowing at your Hara point, the Incarnational star.

Create and re-create this practice daily - ask Divine Mother Source for Her assistance to allow pain to move into Light and it shall be given.

In this way, you shall move and shift your perception and perspective rapidly through layers into higher dimensions. Connecting to your multi-dimensional self. In practising this process of connection to Light much healing and deep insights shall be received.

Opening your akasha is a process which you all can achieve when you are ready to truly see. In opening your akasha you will be aware of your greater self, your multi-dimensional Soul nature as well as your Infinite connection to Divine Mother through the strands of your DNA and at the microcosmic cellular levels of your body.

Through opening your akasha much is re-membered and realised upon the exact nature of your Souls' calling in this present lifetime. Your dharma shall be revealed to you. Once revealed there is no turning back. In resistance to your Soul's calling you will re-create the duality and duplicity experienced currently by many in the 3rd and 4th dimensional funnel. Resistance may come and go - but you will soon know that to reside with the full Light and Love of Divine Mother Creatress is an absolute Joy. Why push such bliss away? Release any residual feelings of being unworthy, of not deserving such bliss. Love and bliss is your Birthright. Know it now, feel it in the very core of your Soul/Heart - connect each day - it is simplicity itself.

Remember that to live with pain and victimhood is to be out of alignment with the nature of Divine Mother. As a Crystal Priestess it is your divine obligation to ensure you are flowing with Light - releasing the burdens of pain as a constant ritual practice. For how can you assist others back to the wholeness of Love and Bliss if you will not release your own pain.

The Crystal Priestess stands firm upon divine Mother Earth/Heart, She is fully grounded in Her Love. She feels and knows the essence of the beautiful energies of the crystal beings with whom she co-creates the journey to wholeness for herself and others. The practise of healing is in all ways co-created weaving a web of Love and Light around and within the Light body of the being to be healed. Healing is a divine ritual, created and held in the sacred space of Love always. The Crystal Priestess acts with Love and absolute reverence for the Crystal Beings as they are in essence a manifestation of Divine Mother always.

~

What more of Ancient Lemuria? So many of you are awakening to the Soul memory of these times and it is a personal and unique energetic shift to you all. Perhaps you feel called to the Sea? You are called to connect with the most ancient parts of Gaia Herself. To the land masses that first emerged from the Oceans - the continent of Pangaea. Perhaps you feel the awakening through communicating with Her plants and of course Her Crystals.

Whatever the nature of your calling, follow your heart. Assist your own journey through daily connection, self-healing and connecting to the Earth/cosmic cycles as they ebb and flow through the Seasons in your location upon the Earth. Remember your soul's origin from the Stars, honour the Beings that reside outside of Earth/Heart and guide you from the Cosmos. They are here to help you and are awaiting acknowledgement from you so that they can communicate to you directly.

Here follows The Memoirs of A Crystal Lover. Reflections on my own atunements to favourite crystal beings. They should be taken as inspiration that speaks to the wisdom within your own Heart.

En-Joy with Love.

Espavo. Rhosalaria - Lady of the Rose Pink Light.

RHOSALARIA GWYNETH ROBBINS-COX

Memoirs of a Crystal Lover

NOTES AND ATUNEMENTS IN CONNECTION TO SOME OF MY FAVOURITE CRYSTALS FOR OUR TIME

These notes are from my own connections with the crystal beings. The picture painted in words of the energies are how the crystals have spoken to me personally. They are free from being a finite definition of the crystal type. Each crystal has its own beautiful story to tell and it will come to you in a way that resonates with your own energy. Therefore these notes are not a prescriptive description of each crystal but an inspirational possibility of what you may feel yourself. Crystal energies are as individual as we are.

ROSE QUARTZ

As I hold my beautiful piece of lavender rose quartz to my heart I immediately sense the warm arms of Mother Earth wrapping around me and a flood of Light and Love flowing through my body cells. I am home. I belong. I sense I am as close to Mother Creatress as I possibly could be in the perception of matter/mater physical Earth and grounding could ever be.

I am here, home, present in the absoulute presence of Her beauty and wisdom. She is holding me so gently and safely in this one moment filling my Soul with Light and infinite Love. She speaks to me of motherly softness - that all is well and that all that is happening is as it is meant to be.

Honouring the physical body. The sheer beauty of being here on Earth Heart now - being who I am and in honouring each and every Soul for their part in Earth's Herstory. We are such infinite beautiful Souls playing out our story of Love and Service now. All is well.

In the presence of Rose, there is no worry - worry is soothed away by Her gentle Light. There is no loneliness for in Her presence we are all One.

She is the essence of Mother Earth pure and simple. Gently, Her Light moves spiralling through my whole Being and where there is sadness - I shed a tear or more - but it is all good. For She holds me through the release to know that it's alright. She holds me in the knowing that sadness and emotional release is all part of the journey to becoming whole. Once sadness is passed - there is nothing but just the sheer elation of Being. The connection to the Earth in Joy.

I hold Her to my womb and I sense the warmth and reassurance that all past lives and future lives, the ancestral timelines are healed and One within infinite love and light. I sense the softness of her divine nurture and holding. Deeper and deeper Her softness and nurture moves through me until I lose the sense of myself and become One with Her purest Love. Just me, the Earth and Rose. All is still and yet gently rocking, cradled like a baby within the softest pink duvet of love.

From this very special love filled still point of grounding and Earth connection I feel free to create and to just purely and simply be me! Anchored to the Love of Creation above and below. Her Light moves through the layers of the physical, emotional, mental energies of my subtle bodies moving outwards, radiating Light to the spiritual bodies and beyond. Like a beacon of Lovelight - sending ripples of Love through the greater conscious awareness of all I am in Soul, beyond and beyond. She weaves Her lovelight to gently release all that is not in alignment with complete self love and self acceptance. How can I be free from completely loving myself when She radiates nothing but the highest unconditional love to me.

She is the mirror of Love, self care, self nurture. From this safe space I am free to love and emanate love through the world and the cosmos. All is Love.

Rhosalaria - July 2021

Rose Quartz copyright G Cox 2021

RUBY

As soon as I hold Ruby and come into Her majestic presence I feel a quickening in my heart! She creates a beautiful warm glow at my centre that sends a beam of love light down through my body to my legs and hips and the Earth Star beneath my feet. From here She enlivens the whole of my Being with the anticipation of Divine Presence - the Omnipresence of Love.

I feel Her sacred flow of fire strengthening all layers of my subtle bodies giving courage in consciousness and direction to my actions, thoughts, feelings and such de-light filled spiritual connection.

Sitting with Ruby I become the Guru. I am my own guru - the teacher within comes to the fore. I sense a divine alignment between the Soul Star awakening the Celestial Tree within the Higher Heart, which then becomes so clear in connection to the Earth Star realising the true grounded manifestation of the Soul upon Earth Heart.

From the Earth Star I sense the fiery passion for life that She awakens rise up through me and I begin to dance upon the Earth in the purest elevated Joy.

Ruby teaches me that all is possible. All is within and just needs a little nurture, passion and compassion to begin to unfurl the petals of potential and manifest the mission of the Soul upon Earth.

She is the passion for life. She is the compassion of the Soul. She encourages the senses, opening to the sensual pleasures of being in a physical body. She is the embodiment of divine sacred tantric union. She opens me to the wisdom of all I am in this lifetime and all the possibilities of who I may be in divine wholeness and sacred Unity. A healing of the timelines of the Soul. She assists forwards movement and simultaneously a quiet contemplation.

Truly She is the embodied presence of the Soul's passion on Earth and the full expression of all that may be. She is the embodiment of the Maitreya/ Christ Consciousness energy awakening Earth Heart now through sacred Light Codes.

With the passion of ruby within my heart I can open to Love and life living my Soul's dream with fulfilment and joy.

Rhosalaria - July 2021

RHOSALARIA GWYNETH ROBBINS-COX

Ruby copyright G Cox 2021

ORANGE SELENITE

Opening to the joyful warm glow of orange selenite I immediately sense the Light of Source stretching out far and beyond and yet contained here within this exquisite crystalline form within my hand.

Holding Her to my heart I sense the embodied joyful web of Light that is within all living things upon the Earth, Sky, within the Earth and beneath the oceans and out into the cosmos.

Within Her luminescence there lies a sense of mystery. The whole story of divine creation held within the Light of Her presence now in crystalline form.

She holds within Her a softness and playfulness that whispers, 'be joyful, celebrate all that you are.' In deeper contemplation with Her, the Light within permeates all my body cells and moves swiftly through my subtle bodies so that I am glowing just as she glows inwardly and outwardly radiating infinite wisdom and joyful knowing. Awakening the ecstatic flow of Light that is within everything.

In connection, She makes me feel a part of the all. The Oneness of spirit and the infinite connection to divinity within and without through Source. As if She holds the key to the mysteries of Life and Creation - She allures me in gentleness and softness and reminds me that we are ever changing beings, not static in form or destiny. We are so much more than what we appear to be! Let's celebrate that!

Soft and almost malleable to the touch She speaks of the transformation and shifting forms of what we call reality. Are we living reality or an illusion? She is wise but teases me with her questioning as She assures me of Her essence present within everything.

She is the Sunset and the Starlight. She is as old as the stardust from which we all come. She is the dawn and the Light of awakening consciousness within each of us. She is the ecstatic flow of life and light.

Rhosalaria - July 2021

THE CRYSTAL SOUL PRIESTESS

Orange Selenite copyright G Cox 2021

GOLDEN HEALER

She draws my gaze inwards to Her beautiful layers of Light and golden hues.

Within the emerging Light of Her depths, I sense and feel the sparks of filaments as if coming together from eons of existence. From across galaxies and universes, like waves and darts of Light particles travelling towards this one time and space to be captured in crystalline form.

She reflects back to me the Light of the Soul. Of all that has been and shall be, captured here in this One moment of radiance. The Light filaments and photons present within my very DNA are awakening to the enlightenment of my Soul's Truth and my mission here.

My own Soul's wisdom and knowing is reflecting to me through Her Light and coming together to be manifest within my core essence. She shows to me how amazing and easy it is to shine my own radiant Light out into the world.

The Light particles within Her reflect the Light in Unity within my own Soular Sun, our Solar Sun and Central Sun, for their essence is One.

Within Her presence I am grounded and whole in who I am. She radiates courage and encouragement radiating a heartfelt confidence in all my conscious actions.

In Her presence I am timeless. I feel the joy and wisdom of lifetimes becoming One within. Like a Shamanic Soul Retrieval she is gathering up the lost pieces in a split second and reassembling them in quantum form.

She tells me that she is an amazing and valuable healer for this time on Earth. Gathering together the fragments of shattered Souls and reconnecting DNA to establish the full awakening of consciousness within as we ascend our frequency into the 5th dimension.

Rhosalaria - July 2021

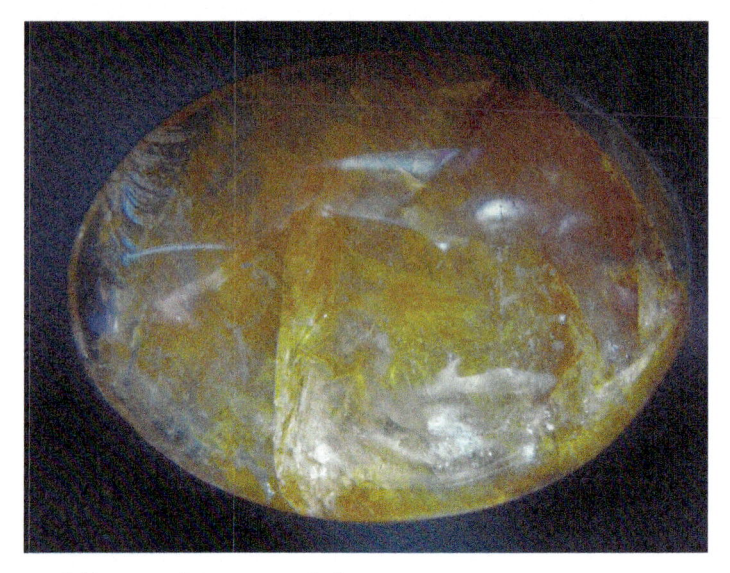

Golden Healer copyright G Cox 2021

DIOPTASE

She sparkles like emerald stars in the night sky. Appearing as individual crystals, tiny and delicate upon her rock matrix. She shows me how One must strive to recognise and to truly live within their sense of sovereignty.

She is unique - She is beautiful. All facets of her sparkle alluring and eluding to the mysterious, the deep unknown expression of who She really is.

She is like an Emerald Goddess of Fire who dares you to show your finest, the beauty of your uniqueness - for this is who She is. Perfect in her sparkling presentation. "Never be afraid to show who you truly are. There are no regrets in life other than opportunities not taken and to walk a path of untruths."

For Her Light demands that you Shine the Light of Truth from your heart constantly and consistently upon your pathway. As you illuminate your own sure steps forwards you also encourage others to do the same.

For who could ignore your dazzling Light when your crystal ally is dioptase.

Rhosalaria - July 2021

Dioptase - copyright G Cox 2021

MALACHITE/ CHRYSOCOLLA

This beautiful stone takes me immediately to a blue/green space of magic within my heart.

I see an altar before me of flowers where I may sit and acknowledge my beauty and honour all that I am.

Sending a prayer to my inner Goddess. I am shown gratitude and appreciation for all that is in my life in this time and space. In this great and beautiful sense of I am presence, I sense deeply the abundance of all that surrounds me.

Feeling the flow of love and creative forces of beauty - of self love and self care and self acceptance. In this one moment of presence, nothing else matters - all is well.

I breathe in beauty and I breathe out appreciation and gratitude for all in Divine presence and grace.

Rhosalaria - July 2021

RHOSALARIA GWYNETH ROBBINS-COX

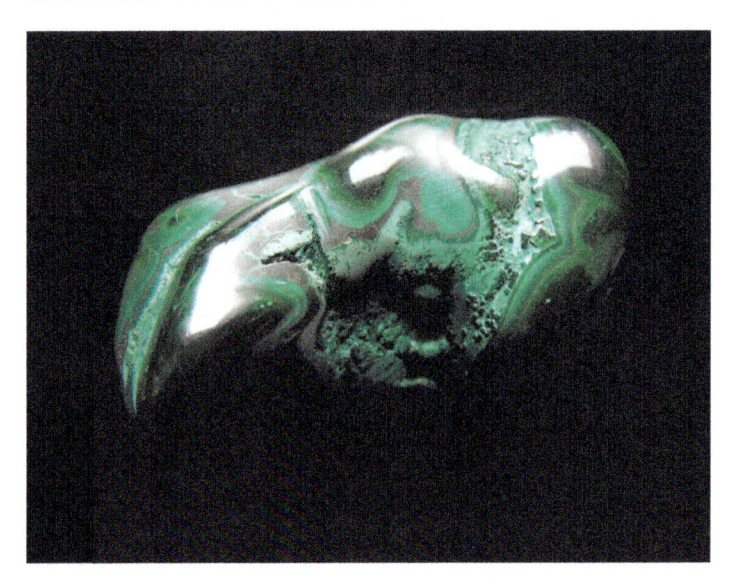

Malachite and Chrysocolla copyright G. Cox 2021

MORGANITE

Her wispy soft breathe of pale pink light wraps around me and pulls me inwards towards her. I am within her. I am part of her, she is part of me.

Within her love light I sense calm and grace. Such delicate Light but powerful and holding. She is gently reassuring me as She delicately elevates my energies upwards. Spiralling up to connect to the purest Light of Source.

Her essence is exquisite. Like a sweet smelling flower, jasmine or honeysuckle, she nurtures the Light within me. Within Her connection there is no separation from the Divine Light for she holds me in such delightful contentment and calmness that all else fades away in insignificance.

She is the Light of my Soul within the Celestial Tree, the Higher Heart and She opens it so carefully so that the Joy I feel will not be lost or dwindled in any way at all.

She brings to me the purest sense of Love light connection that reassures me that all is well. In this divine connection she encourages me upon my path of Light and Love. Integrating all grace and knowingness. I am wrapped within Her subtlety and strength.

If I listen carefully I can hear her say, 'there you are, you knew that you could do it all along.' She is the softest courage and encouragement within the Light. She is the breathe of Love and Grace in Crystalline Form.

Rhosalaria - July 2021

Morganite copyright G Cox 2021

AQUAMARINE

Connecting with this beautiful crystal is like the flow of light from above washing through me like a waterfall of cleansing Light.

She is connection to Divine Source in words and feelings and complete in-spiration.

As I begin to unfold my intentions to flow with Her Light I realise the synchronicity she holds within her.

'Be with me,' she says, 'and I will help you to see and vision with great clarity and flow. You shall know exactly where to be. In the right time and the right place all unfolds within the grace and flow of Divine Mother Source.'

For there are no coincidences with Aquamarine. She shall harness the power of your Souls Light to see clearly your direction. To speak your Truth with clarity and purpose. She shall open your inner vision and listening to see and communicate far beyond your usual periphery.

With aquamarine you shall flow through the rivers of clear sight and become the visionary of your own destiny and purpose in alignment with your Soul's mission.

She shall so deftly wash away all that is not needed within the subtle bodies of your Being whilst holding you and protecting you within the divine inspiration that constantly flows through you. Awakening to your greater consciousness - She is the crystal visionary of Inspiration, Clarity and Truth.

Rhosalaria - July 2021

THE CRYSTAL SOUL PRIESTESS

Blue Aquamarine copyright G Cox 2021

LARIMAR

As I first hold Larimar to my heart, She makes me smile.

Oh ocean Goddess of such depth and Unity.

She is Domnu, Yemanye the Ocean Queen Mother of life itself. Ancient One - keeper of deep secrets, within you lies the essence - the eau de vie - the secrets of Life itself.

She flows around me in her deep energy of wisdom. Like the whales and the dolphins She holds so much knowledge of Earth Heart. The stories of old and the Truths still yet untold - and within Her connection She teases and gives me little pieces of Truth and stories that draw me in to the immense Unity that is the collective Sea of Consciousness.

Yet She reflects to me the Joy of all that is for the visions She creates for me are of the Golden life giving energy of the Sun sparkling on crystal clear blue seas. What would we be without the Light and heat of the Sun and the flow of the life giving waters?

In such reflection She shows me that we are all part

of the One, part of the Whole - we all hold within us the keys to Life and Light and Love. From Love and Light we came and to that we shall return.

Oh sweet Ocean Mother - Larimar - you encourage such Love and Strength in your connection. The reflection of who we are as hue-manity. You are the essence, the carrier of our consciousness.

Let us love you and reflect back to you the love you give over and over. Wave after wave of Love Divine. A reflection of our Divine Mother Creatress - we are One.

Rhosalaria July 2021

RHOSALARIA GWYNETH ROBBINS-COX

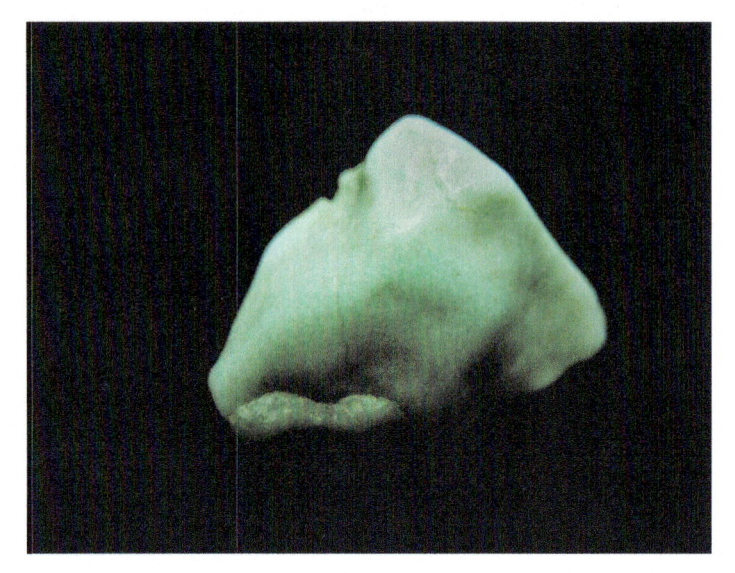

Larimar copyright G Cox 2021

CHAROITE

As Charoite wraps Her calming energies around me like a dark cloak of purple I am led into a vision.

I see Her, like a friend, a calm and trusting Priestess of old holding out Her hand to me as we walk a long and narrow tree lined pathway. The end of the path is never in view - the path stretches on seemingly into eternity. The trees hug each other as they bend forwards touching gently to create a tunnel.

Within this tree lined tunnel pathway I feel safe. I am led always forwards by the Priestess of Charoite in front. There are no turns and the feelings are of security and righteousness and virtue. This is a pathway of dedication. As such a spiritual dedication that I'm aware is sometimes rocky with the allure of diversions - and yet there is no going back.

Every now and then it seems as though we travel through doorways and the Light towards the end of the tunnel becomes more intense. As we pass through these doorways I am gifted an extra sense of knowing and wisdom and surety that all is well and as it should be.

Charoite inspires and helps me remember who I am. Through her unwavering dedication to the Path - I am gifted the deepest insights in reflection of my own awakening. Remembering the wisdoms of the past perhaps hidden till now. The deepest Soul Wisdoms to help carry me onwards diligently and silently with ease.

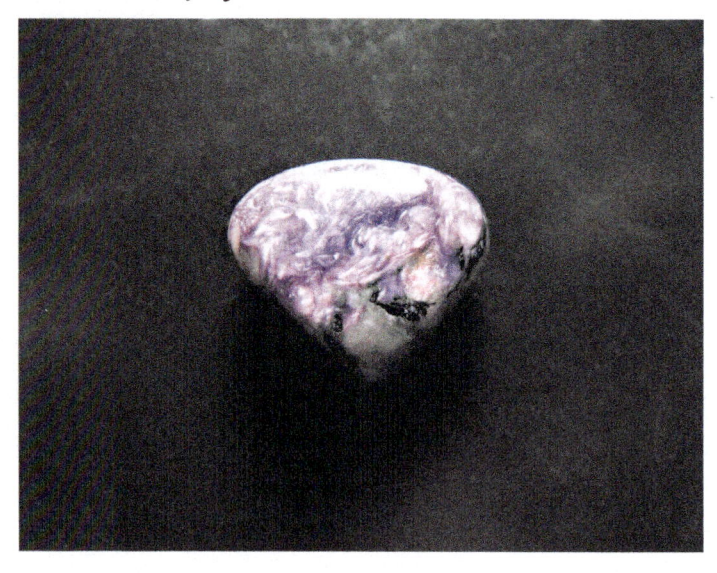

Rhosalaria - July 2021

Charoite copyright G Cox 2021

LEMURIAN PINK QUARTZ

She is the Temple of Light at the Centre of my Heart. So ancient and beautiful she sparkles Her wisdom to me in the deepest and most flowing outpouring of Love and Remembering.

She is the channel of Light for messages from Divine Mother Creatress. She is the purest Light of Source.

In vision I behold the Rose Temple of Light and upon the altar of Love and Light I am offered the reflective mirror of all that has been and all that shall be - entrance into the Universal Heart of the Akasha.

Waves of Love emanate through Her, unlocking the mysteries of past and future Being and little by little I see the reflection of it all in the One moment of presence.

She is a Divine Amplifier of remembering all that was lost in the times of Lemuria and a great keeper of such immense Divine Cosmic Love and Light.

The Ancient wisdoms are held within Her for safe-keeping and only those who are open, through willing hearts may hear her Light Language of Love as She sings out the Ancient Soul Songs of remembering.

Through Her songs she speaks of homecoming, of Unity and restoration. Through Her we may hear the whispers of wisdom that shall be grounded within the creation of New Earth. She upholds the common unity of Love as the Rise of Divine Feminine and Divine Masculine as One in the emerging of New Earth and the Golden Age.

She is simply love, light and inspiration.

Rhosalaria, July 2021

Lemurian Pink Quartz copyright G Cox 2021

CELESTITE

So soft and delicate are the energies of celestite. As I hold her carefully and feel Her delicacy and softness I am feeling and sensing the presence of Angels.

So high up, I am spiralling to be enfolded within their arms. The delicate drusy nature of celestite reflected within the delicate touch of Angels Wings.

I am within the higher realms of all possibilities - I see to the distance, a small point of Light, the Ain Soph - the place of limitless Light from whence all matter is first dreamed.

She permeates my Being with a softness and calmness that is otherworldly. A memory between incarnations of such existence. As if between dreams She whispers that dreams are but the reflections of my consciousness. She assures me that she shall help me remember the dreams of my souls memory and bring them into the Light of consciousness. She assures me that through my dreaming I can remember and bring through the greatest potentials and possibilities from my Souls essence.

For She is the softest Light of that which has been and all that which may come to be if we engage our faith and trust.

She is the guide who comes to us in our dreams to calm and soothe our worries away with the lightest touch - have trust and faith in Her now as her softest most ethereal Light Rays permeate your dreaming by day and night. She holds the keys to manifestation of Peace on Earth.

She is the Ethereal Temple of Dreaming where we may learn to trust and have faith in the Light and our potential. Listen carefully to Her soft words of wisdom - you will need to open your heart and mind fully to hear, so ethereal is She you could just miss Her whispers. Entrain your energy to Hers and you shall enjoy the most peaceful calm and entry to the deepest field of Divine Mind.

Rhosalaria - July 2021

Celestite copyright G Cox 2021

SOPHIA STONE

'I am the gatekeeper to the wisdoms of the Earth.'

'I am the ethereal spirit of Mother Gaia herself. Her ancient wisdoms and beauty are open to you only if you open your heart truly to the energies I am emanating to you now.'

In my connection to Her I see the vastness of the Earth and I see that She is the watcher of all huemankind.

Her eyes are wide open to huemanity and to the story of our healing. She seeks to purify and to heal us as She elevates Her own resonant frequencies, She watches the destruction and self destruction that huemanity wreaks upon the Earth and all Living Beings. She is sad yet remains hopeful for She carries the knowledge and knowing of the Stars and the Destiny of Earth.

She offers grounding and imbues a sense of Sovereignty and patience in the knowledge that all is written within Cosmic Law and the stars themselves, that Huemanity will rise into ascension to be the Light Beings they are destined to be.

She watches - She holds the space - She offers

healing through the deep purifying energies of the Earth. She is the Divine nurturing Mother and in Her ever watchful patience awaits the rise of the Divine Feminine as She returns to the conscious awareness of Her children.

Rhosalaria - July 2021

Sophia Stone copyright G Cox 2021

CARNELIAN

She calls me to hold her and bring her to my womb space. Within just a few breaths I am feeling her fiery flame energy as it fills my body and Soul.

Connecting to my inner wisdom - the knowing of lifetimes, I feel her purifying and letting go of the stories and narratives of the past. She takes me back through the echoes of my Soul's memory, to the visions of times passed. Those memories of strength and those wherein lie the 'patterns' of duality within. The drama and the trauma of the past - echoing and yet now being purified in her orange/white flame of purification. She is my protection and my strength.

Gently She brings me back into focus, into complete presence and with motivation and without doubt to co-create with her and step forwards, continuing upon the path of Light with fiery passion - with self belief and inner strength.

She allows the visions of creation to unfold gently but with true purpose in my mind and I am able to see and feel the frequency clearly with love and a heart free of clouded judgements. For all is and shall ever be a co-creation of passion with love and grace.

Rhosalaria - July 2021

Carnelian Flame copyright G Cox 2021

BOTROIYDAL GRAPE AMETHYST

Holding this unique and beautiful grape amethyst to my heart, I am immediately uplifted onto a plane of joy and peacefulness. Holding me in such complete presence I am now feeling the gentle and playful energies of this beautiful crystal.

Through such presence, peace and joy - I sense the violet transformation that says, ' I am a crystal for your time. There are no boundaries, let yourself fly! The only boundaries are the ones you create for yourself.'

The violet light moves outwards like a radar pulsing, emanating light, spiritual connection, love, joy and all in complete presence.

'I am all and yet a part of the whole. Individual and collective as you are too. We are one - and together we create New Earth with new innovations, new ideas, new beginnings.

The past is gone - why worry about it. All you have is now and I am here to help you move forwards with a sense of rejuvenation within your spirit. We are in the 5th dimension now - drop the dualities of the past - these times are long gone.

Hold me to your higher heart and I will help you feel the joy of the Celestial tree within your Soul - hold me to your third eye and you will see a new reality. It is here - the time is now.'

Rhosalaria - July 2021

Botroidal Grape Amethyst copyright G Cox 2021

BLUE MOSS CHALCEDONY

I am whisked away in a blue ethereal energy that lifts me upwards towards the sky.

As I am transported I sense the letting go of illusions. Illusions are like the clouds - ethereal , thoughts of no matter - and I sigh with a deep letting go and relief.

Further and further we spiral upwards through the pale blue into the true limitless reality of spirit and Source - connecting to the Limitless Light - the boundless - the Ain Soph potential of all things that may become matter. A place of thoughts and dreams.

Here in the space of dreams - we are connected to the devas of Air - the ethereal fae world of no matter. In this place I am shown that I can shift swiftly through self-limiting beliefs and that which holds me captive and heavy. In this place I am boundless - just energy - expansive - ethereal.

Within this temple space of boundless energies -

I am reminded that all is One with Source, and we are connecting to the Source of all creation - the wholeness of everything - within and without. From this place we may flow with the perception of our own Trust and Faith. For now I see through the delusions into limitless dimensions of possibility. All is well in this true heavenly space and yet there is a groundedness within this space. Whence we feel such boundlessness - we are truly present within the all seeing eye of Divine Mother Creatress herself who holds us safe.

Rhosalaria July 2021

Blue Moss Chalcedony copyright G Cox 2021

PREHNITE

Prehnite comes to me like the essence of dew on a soft spring morning. Refreshing me she beams her radiant fine essence of Light through my heart and soular plexus - and she reminds me to not hurry.

'There is no time. No need for stress or anxiousness. Time is curved and you are here with me in the now - breathe in my essence and all is well. I shall renew all that you are.' I feel the beams of light penetrating my Soul's energy - deep at my core - reminding me of who I am and what I came here to do and to be.

I am free from giving in to anything other than that which is my true calling and that which serves my highest essence. Gently confident - for there are no loud exuberances here within the energy of prehnite. Just being - free from the connections to inner chatter and inner dramas. All is renewed and refreshed moment by moment until at last, I am like a beautiful pale green star - shining brightly in my own space. Comfortable within my own space and prehnite promises to remind me of all I am gently whenever there are doubts and the outside world is in chaos.

Within the worldly being of prehnite all is recreated in love, radiance, freshness and delight - all is calm and at peace in wholeness within itself.

Rhosalaria - July 2021

Prehnite   copyright G Cox 2021

LABRADORITE

I am the time traveller of space and the multidimensional nature of your Soul.

Connecting to labradorite energies we are at one within ourselves and the multi faceted world of our Soul's Being - all lives past and future at once. Sensing the shifting energies of wisdoms weaving like a luxurious pearlescent thread throughout all the realities and dimensions of who we truly are. Our Soul's essence.

Feeling into the heart - we are all these beings at once. All that we are within the centre of the heart. We are one and all.

For once the movement of the timeless threads of reality come together within the heart centre, I am strong with the most secure boundaries. For in this space at the centre of the heart - I am me - I know myself fully. I am, that I am.

Labradorite calls us to journey once more and to gather up those threads of memories past. Some good and some not so good but it is all part of who we are and we must accept it all in love and grace for Labradorite shows us the shimmering mirror of our Truth - past and present, future and present - we are whole and yet secure within the expansiveness of our vast Soul Consciousness. As such we are all One, all hue-manity as a collective and beautiful network of conscious connection. A network of love and light.

Rhosalaria July 2021

Labradorite copyright G Cox 2021

ANANDALITE

She calls me to her starry sky studded with brilliant white Light. As I hold Her it is like holding starlight in my hands. She is radiantly beautiful.

Her Light radiates outwards from my heart in all directions until I feel like a star. Expanding the Light through my subtle bodies outwards through my aura - expanding in a boundless web of Light.

Outwards and outwards as though connecting to the stars themselves. I journey with Her and begin to see what it is she is showing me - the boundless reality of the Universe, the Cosmos and yet, all that which is reflected and is contained within the tiniest cell within my body. Macro and micro.

I feel the connection to the great web of Souls within the Stars. She truly is the Star Goddess - Anandalite - my star companion. She shows me there are no boundaries and yet all is connected. She shows me the subtleties of nature - She is the One - She is the whole and She is the One who weaves the web of Souls - with Her fine Light radiating and reflecting/refracting the purest white

Light. She is Divine Integration. All is contained within Her - all is reflected through me. She is the Light of Source and source is within me.

Rhosalaria - July 2021

Anandalite   copyright G Cox 2021

ELESTIAL SMOKY QUARTZ

My faithful friend. Elestial smoky quartz will tell me no lies. She is inscrutably truthful - there is nowhere to hide from her wisdoms.

Within Her presence One is called to be humble and still. To listen carefully with open heart and open third eye - opening to the emotional intelligence within. For sitting with Her I find the deepest and wisest truths of myself and all situations that have been co-created. The sadness of loss and disappointment that is my own doing when I have not listened to the Truth within. For this Elestial Angel represents the greatest of truths.

She is free from being too harsh and her soft voice ripples through me. I hold her close and I feel the softness of Angelic wings enfolding around me. For in connection to her - I am in unity with the Angel within myself.

She speaks to me as a kind grandmother, reminding me of that which I have forgotten and of that which I have yet to remember and integrate within me. She is the Angelic mirror of myself.

She holds me and protects me within the essence of my Truth. Connecting to the crystalline matrix of Light reflected within the crystalline body that is mine - she shows me the Angelic inner seeds - the Starchild within that is rebirthing from within me now.

She offers the greatest of blessings at this time of Ascension - She blesses you One and All upon your great journey Homewards - Starbeings of Earth Heart.

'You are the Angelic Beings you were meant to be. The Inner Child is healed. The Angel is integrated fully in Unity with Divine Feminine and Divine Masculine. So it is. So it shall be.'

Espavo. Om Shanti. Blessed Be.

Rhosalaria - July 2021

Elestial Smoky Quartz   copyright G Cox 2021

CRYSTALLINE TRANSMISSIONS

Here are Just a few images of Crystalline Transmissions of Love and Light. Within each crystalline grid attention is given to the energy frequencies created by the number of crystals, the type of crystals and the colour vibration of the crystals. Each brings a resonance that weaves together an overall frequency to create a unique crystalline transmission. Intention and intuition is all.

Lemurian Blessings of Light and Love - rose quartz, lemurian quartz, rose aura quartz and Caribbean calcite with pink roses.   copyright G Cox 2020

RHOSALARIA GWYNETH ROBBINS-COX

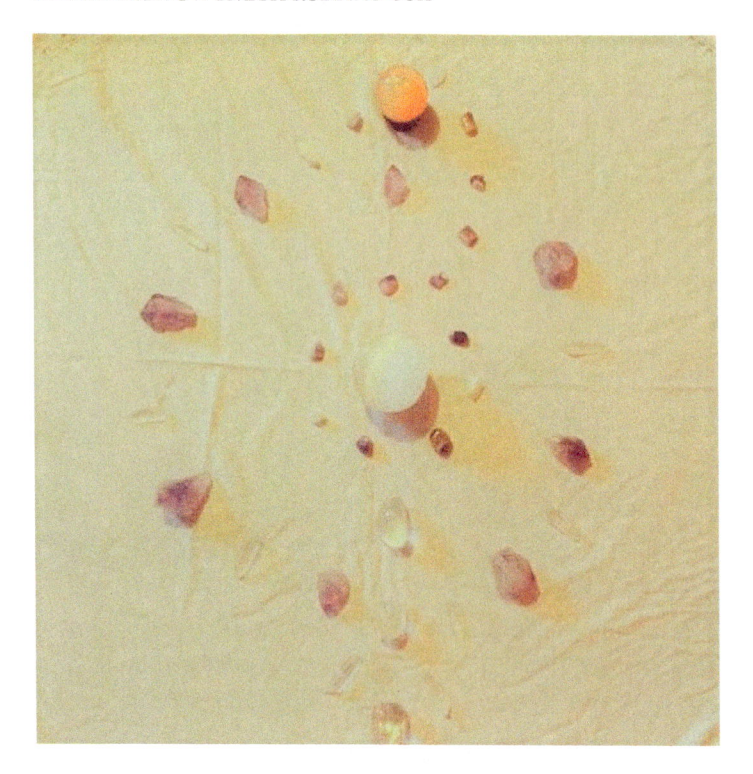

Violet flame grid with amethyst and lemurian quartz and the source energies of selenite and orange selenite. For the partial full moon eclipse in November 2021

Lemurian Spiral of Light. Remembering the Lemurian Soul bringing Light and Healing through the heart centre to the Soul. Amethyst points, turquoise and citrine. July 2018

RHOSALARIA GWYNETH ROBBINS-COX

Swirling mandala of black agates and red garnets to remove negative energy in the environment and the aura and promote positivity and change. May 2021 copyright G Cox 2021

Part of a large Crystal Mandala - Connection to Source

Celestite, Selenites, Opalites, Afghanite, Blue Obsidian, Angelite, Aquamarine

Crystals for Consciousness workshop at The Malindi Centre, Carmarthenshire July 2019

All photographs within this book are the unique and copyright credited to Gregory Cox and Rhosalaria Gwyneth Robbins-Cox

Cover image is copyrighted and created by Pia Tohveri PhD - please visit her website at Piatohveri.com

For details on Crystal Soul Healing courses and other Crystal Healing Courses please go to Mycrystalguru.com

For events, Soul Guidance Reading from the Akasha and healing sessions please go to Heartandsoulhorizons.com

The 12 chakra/aura diagram is credited to my daughter Kara McGlinn.

AFTERWORD

Thank you for reading this book. I hope you enjoyed it.

Crystals can offer us so much love and light in these changing times.

The channelled information contained here is a large part of the story and I have been free from editing the words that came through so as to preserve the essence of love that was intended to be read.

ABOUT THE AUTHOR

Rhosalaria Gwyneth Robbins-Cox

The author is a healer, soul medium, teacher and priestess of avalon.

She teaches Crystal Soul Healing through Crystal Heart School and Soul Mediumship through Heart and Soul Horizons.

She has also written childrens books, The Shimmering Sea written for her granddaughter Anwen, which is available on Amazon.

She is dedicated to the creative inspiration that working with crystal brings and believes in nurturing the inner healer within us all.

Printed in Great Britain
by Amazon